Fast
Scaling

ISBN: 978-3-00-068214-8 (Print)
ISBN: 978-3-00-068215-5 (E-Book)

First Edition 1 2 3 4 5 6 7 8 9 10

GROWTH HANDBOOK
FOR FOUNDERS

Fast Scaling

The Smart Path to Building
Massively Valuable
Businesses

PATRICK FLESNER

To:

Cosima Catharina
Felix Joe
Lina Sophie
Milla Luise
Nina

Contents

FASTSCALING   153

Chapter 9

Focusing on Customer Success   155

Chapter 10

Growing Predictably   177

Chapter 11

Growing Efficiently   189

Chapter 12

Leading a High Growth Organization   201

Together with my partners at LeadX Capital Partners, I have built one of the biggest European portfolios of tech companies active in consumer industries. Each year, I look at hundreds of B2B and B2C businesses that want to accelerate growth. I see many patterns in companies that fail and companies that succeed. My respective expertise as well as my knowledge and experience from more than fifteen years in Private Equity, Venture Capital, and M&A have gone into this book.

This book is for you if you are a founder or an aspiring founder who wants to build a massively valuable high growth business and become a highly effective growth leader sufficiently proficient in every growth discipline. Reading this book will enable you to become a strong leader who sets the right north star, asks the correct questions, and zooms in on all material issues related to growing your business. In this book, you will learn why, when, and how to Fast-Scale. Strategy and execution.

You may find your smart path to building a massively valuable business.

Patrick Flesner

How to Use This Book

This book is meant to show you a smart and systematic path to building massively valuable businesses. As the chapters systematically build on each other, I recommend you read this book straight through from the introduction to the end.

Reading chapter by chapter will enable you to fully understand why FastScaling means more than just growing your top line in terms of revenue. You will see why it makes sense to first establish a solid high growth foundation and then FastScale.

If you follow the system, you cannot only achieve high growth and a massive valuation. As you scale cash efficiently, you can also retain a higher stake in your company.

After having embraced the FastScaling methodology, you can also use this book as a reference whenever you want to dive deeper into specific high growth topics.

You will find additional resources, videos, blog posts and updates on my website fastscaling.io. Please subscribe to the blog and be informed about new blog posts and additional relevant content.

Introduction

Great articles and books have been written about how to start companies as well as specific growth topics like getting to product/market fit, getting traction, generating predictable revenue, accelerating sales, and leading growth. These are great resources you can refer to if you want to become more proficient in distinct growth-related areas of your business.

As a growth capital investor, I have read many of the respective articles, blog posts, and books. Relevant ideas and advice have directly or indirectly found their way into this book. I have referenced these resources under Notes and Resources.

As a founder, however, you need to be sufficiently proficient in every growth discipline. If you want to lead your organization successfully, you need to be sufficiently proficient in marketing, sales, customer success, product, engineering, finance, and business intelligence. While strong leadership does not derive solely from knowledge, outstanding professional competence will not only strengthen your self-confidence, but also your credibility. With a strong cross-functional expertise, your employees will more likely trust your judgments and decisions.

Providing you with this cross-functional expertise and a smart strategy to building massively valuable businesses is the goal of this book.

Keep in mind, however, that each and every startup is different. Every founder has to make her own decision in terms of when and how to scale her company.

I have written this book especially for founders who are looking for a systematic path to scaling their businesses. Founders who question whether every startup needs to be scaled with a relentless focus on top line growth. Founders who feel that they might be better off pursuing a fast, but less aggressive, approach to growth. If you are such a founder looking for a systematic, fast, and smart approach to growing your business, this book is for you.

Unless market dynamics require you to prioritize speed over efficiency, you can FastScale. It may take you a bit longer. But the probability that you will succeed is significantly higher.

Patrick Flesner

Introduction to FastScaling

CHAPTER 1

Premature Scaling, Blitzscaling, & FastScaling

There's nothing wrong with raising venture capital. Many lean startups are ambitious and are able to deploy large amounts of capital. What differentiates them is their disciplined approach to determining when to spend money: after the fundamental elements of the business model have been empirically validated.[1]

ERIC RIES, AUTHOR OF 'THE LEAN STARTUP'

As a founder, you call the shots.

You choose the problem that you want to solve, your target market, and the co-founders who embark with you on this challenging and exciting journey. You make the first hires who are so incredibly important for your company culture. You

[1] The Lean Startup – How Today's Entrepreneurs Use Continuous Innovation to Create Radically Successful Businesses / by Eric Ries.

are the leader who sets the north star and ensures your strategy is being executed.

You are not only the founder, but also the Chief Scalability Officer. You must establish how your company achieves high growth readiness. You must decide how much money to raise and choose your investors. If your company has already generated initial traction, you need to decide when, and how, to fuel the growth engine and accelerate growth, a major decision many founders struggle with.

In 2011, a Startup Genome Report, which was co-authored by researchers from UC Berkeley and Stanford, surveyed 3,200 startups in order to better understand what makes high growth technology startups succeed and fail. The results were astonishing:

- 70% of startups failed because of premature scaling.

- Startups that scaled properly grew about 20 times faster than startups that scaled prematurely.[2]

Premature scaling comes in many shapes and forms. You overspend on customer acquisition before you have found product/market fit. You invest heavily in growth before you have found a channel that lets you acquire customers efficiently. You hire too many employees… and too fast. Essentially, you burn unnecessary amounts of cash before you have validated the fundamental elements of your business model. This is a template for failure.

2   A Deep Dive Into The Anatomy Of Premature Scaling / by Startup Genome. Retrieved from: https://startupgenome.com/blog/a-deep-dive-into-the-anatomy-of-premature-scaling-new-infographic.

A specific form of premature scaling is blitzscaling. Reid Hoffman and Chris Yeh coined the term 'blitzscaling' for an approach to growth that prioritizes speed over efficiency in the face of uncertainty.[3] You make decisions before you know exactly how things will play out. You accept the risk of making mistakes and operating inefficiently, in exchange for moving faster. You start scaling without having proven that your business model actually works. It is like drawing to an inside straight. When you hit, you win huge, but most of the time you will lose.

FastScaling - On the basis of a relentless and company-wide focus on customer success, product/market-fit, product/channel-fit, strong unit economics, and a scalable technology infrastructure, efficiently and predictably leading and scaling a business fast towards market leadership in a large market.

Some founders have indeed managed to blitzscale their businesses successfully. Hoffman and Yeh mention, among others, the founders of Airbnb, Alibaba, Amazon, Dropbox, Facebook, LinkedIn, Netflix, PayPal, Slack, Spotify, and Stripe.

It is undeniable that this aggressive approach to growth has worked well for these founders. And it may be tempting to emulate their blitzscaling approach. But blitzscaling is by no means

---

3   Blitzscaling : the lightning-fast path to creating massively valuable businesses / by Reid Hoffman and Chris Yeh.

the right strategy for each and every founder. The contrary is true. Hoffman and Yeh emphasize that blitzscaling means disregarding many of the normal rules of business and comes with an abnormally high risk of failure. They make it loud and clear that it makes sense to blitzscale only if speed into the market is *the* critical strategy to achieve massive outcomes.[4]

Until you reach this strategic inflection point where you need to prioritize speed over efficiency, you can avoid any form of premature scaling and pursue the FastScaling approach described in this book. If you FastScale, you carefully balance speed and efficiency. Ultimately, it may take you a bit longer. But the probability that you succeed building a massively valuable business is significantly higher.

The FastScaling methodology consists of two distinct growth phases.

You establish the FastScaling foundation that validates the viability of your business model. You generate product/market fit and product/channel fit. You ensure your technology is stable, secure, and scalable. You strive for market leadership in a sufficiently large market.

If your growth readiness is reflected in strong unit economics, you FastScale. You focus relentlessly on customer success. You generate predictable revenue and scale cash efficiently. You demonstrate strong leadership skills and create a successful high growth organization.

4   The pioneers of Silicon Valley's fast culture on how to grow quickly, not recklessly / by Reid Hoffman and Chris Yeh. Retrieved from: https://qz.com/1572866/reid-hoffman-and-chris-yeh-defend-their-book-blitzscaling/.

• • • • •

If you consider pursuing a smart path to building a massively valuable business or want to get from initial traction to sustainable high growth, turn to Chapter 2. In Chapter 2, we will start with an overview of the five FastScaling building blocks you need to establish in order to accelerate growth on the basis of a solid high growth foundation.

Key Founder Takeaways

☐ 70% of startups fail because of premature scaling. Startups that scale properly grow about 20 times faster than startups that scale prematurely.

☐ Premature scaling comes in many shapes and forms. Essentially, you burn unnecessary amounts of cash before you have validated the fundamental elements of your business model.

☐ A specific form of premature scaling is blitzscaling. If you blitzscale you make decisions before you know exactly how things will play out. You accept the risk of making mistakes and operating inefficiently, in exchange for moving faster.

☐ Until you reach the strategic inflection point where you need to prioritize speed over efficiency, you can avoid any form of premature scaling. You can FastScale.

☐ If you FastScale, you carefully balance speed and efficiency. Ultimately, it may take you a bit longer. But the probability that you succeed building a massively valuable business is significantly higher.

☐ FastScaling: On the basis of a relentless and company-wide focus on customer success, product/market-fit, product/channel-fit, strong unit economics and a scalable technology infrastructure, efficiently and predictably leading and scaling a business fast towards market leadership in a large market.

☐ The FastScaling methodology consists of two distinct growth phases.

☐ You establish the FastScaling foundation that validates the viability of your business model. You generate product/market fit and product/channel fit. You ensure that your technology is stable, secure, and scalable. You aim at achieving market leadership in a sufficiently large market.

☐ If your growth readiness is reflected in strong unit economics, you FastScale. You focus relentlessly on customer success. You generate predictable revenue and scale cash efficiently. You demonstrate strong leadership skills and create a successful high growth organization.

CHAPTER 2

Establishing the FastScaling Foundation

I am a fan of the slow and steady approach to building a business. I call it crawl, walk, run. Crawl, walk, run is more resilient. It allows for mistakes that aren't fatal. It takes a bit longer to get to the finish line this way, but the probability of success is way higher with crawl, walk, run. Crawl, walk, run is a mantra for doing a startup and I recommend it to everyone.[5]

FRED WILSON, MANAGING PARTNER AT UNION SQUARE VENTURES

E very success is the result of a combination of hard work and luck. But, if you do not work hard, you will definitely fail. Or, put differently, the harder you work the luckier you get.

Focusing on top line growth only and hoping all the other pieces will fall into place over time is nothing but a shortcut. Do not look for shortcuts! With every shortcut you increase the portion of luck you need to succeed. Instead, work harder to build a solid

5   Crawl, Walk, Run / by Fred Wilson. Retrieved from: https://avc.com/2020/07/crawl-walk-run/.

growth foundation. Then, you can scale fast, predictably, efficiently, and eventually successfully.

I have realized that many of the founders who managed to create sustainable high growth companies worked hard on establishing five fundamental growth building blocks before they accelerated growth. They focused on generating product/market fit and creating a working distribution channel to their key target customers. They penetrated a large target market. All this in place, they could fuel the growth engine on the basis of strong unit economics reflecting a viable business model. Some, however, failed anyway, burned unnecessary amounts of cash, or lost precious time, because they did not ensure their technology infrastructure could cope with the significant increase in traffic and usage that came with long periods of high growth. Fixing such technology issues was always tremendously expensive, even disregarding opportunity costs, and led to severe drops in morale and enthusiasm among employees who had been hired to accelerate growth or had been working hard in order to create a solid growth basis.

*FastScaling - On the basis of a relentless and company-wide focus on customer success, **product/market-fit, product/channel-fit, strong unit economics, and a scalable technology infrastructure**, efficiently and predictably leading and scaling a business fast towards market leadership in a **large market**.*

I have translated these insights into the five FastScaling building blocks that must be in place before you heavily invest in growth. The

FastScaling foundation consists of: product/market fit, product/channel fit, a large target market, strong unit economics, and a stable, secure, and scalable technology infrastructure.

Even if you are a founder who leads a business with already significant initial traction, I encourage you to read the chapters about creating a solid growth foundation. You should double check whether you have indeed achieved high growth readiness. On top, topics like generating product/market and product/channel fit are by no means topics relevant only for early-stage companies. They are relevant throughout the lifecycle of a business and especially when it comes to accelerating growth. Do not get overconfident in this regard!

Generating Product/Market Fit

Marc Andreessen, the co-founder and general partner at Andreessen Horowitz, once famously said: "The only thing that matters is product/market fit."[6] While product/market fit is only one pillar of the FastScaling foundation, it indeed matters a lot.

Product/market fit has been achieved if your products solve a significant customer problem and satisfy a market need. If you do not find product/market fit and invest in growth, you sell products nobody needs. To be clear, generating revenue does not mean that you have found product/market fit. I have seen too many founders who asked their sales force to push products into the market in

6   Product/Market Fit / by Marc Andreessen: Retrieved from: https://web.stanford.edu/class/ee204/ProductMarketFit.html.

order to generate growth. This approach was unsustainable. Newly acquired customers churned[7] fast or never returned. Completely dissatisfied customers left bad reviews that prevented other customers from buying. A vicious circle that often led to complete failure.

In an interview, Fred Wilson pointed out that early traction must not be a sign for having found product/market fit: "A hard charging, sales-oriented founder/CEO can often hide the defects in a product. Because the founder is so capable of convincing the market to adopt/purchase the product, the company can get revenue traction with a product that is not really right."[8]

Product/market fit is the proof you sell something that is of significant value to your target customers. The value you create translates into a high willingness to pay and a compelling contribution per customer. Your economics work.

Pets.com is a company that is sometimes referred to as a company that scaled prematurely without having found product/market fit. Pets.com was a dot-com company that sold pet food and accessories online. Cutting out the middlemen, the Pets.com pitch to customers was based on convenience. Pet owners could order online pet products that were conveniently delivered directly to the homes of the pet owners.

But before validating that this solution was actually solving a real customer pain or, at least, a customer problem that pet owners

---

7   Churn means that your customers who pay monthly, quarterly, or yearly fees terminate their contracts and do not have to pay any license fee anymore.

8   11 Lessons From Venture Capitalist Fred Wilson / by CB Insights. Retrieved from: https://www.cbinsights.com/research/report/venture-capital-lessons-fred-wilson/.

were willing to pay for, the founders raised huge amounts of venture capital and invested in marketing campaigns. Online, print, radio, and television, including a Superbowl TV commercial. While the marketing investments led to great customer awareness, demand remained moderate and significantly behind expectations. In economic terms, this meant little traction in the acquisition of new customers and revenue growth. Customers who tried Pets.com could not be retained. There was not yet a need for the Pets.com service in the market. Correspondingly, the economics did not work. What followed was a huge cash burn and a complete business shut down after only two years. Allegedly, Pets.com burned through $300m.

Generating product/market fit is not only relevant when you start a venture. It remains relevant at any and all times, particularly if you want to accelerate growth. Growth acceleration often comes hand in hand with expanding your product offering, penetrating new markets, or selling to new customer segments. In all these situations, you need to generate product/market fit before you invest heavily in the distribution of your products and services.

We discuss how to generate and measure product/market fit in Chapter 4.

Generating Product/Channel Fit

Product/market fit is necessary. You need to get to product/market fit before you accelerate growth. But what good is product/market fit if you cannot sell your products on attractive economic terms? No working distribution channel, no success.

In their book 'Traction', Gabriel Weinberg and Justin Mares explore nineteen channels startups can use to reach their target customers. [9] And there are many more potential channels. Do not disregard any channel as irrelevant! As Peter Thiel, founder of Pay-Pal and Founder Fund, rightfully stressed in his book 'Zero To One': "Most businesses get zero distribution channels to work. If you try for several but don't nail one, you're finished." [10]

If you FastScale, you go through a long period of high growth. You therefore need to find not only channels through which you can sell your products. You need to find scalable channels through which you can continuously sell your products on attractive economic terms. Channels that allow you to continuously increase the number of customers predictably and sustainably. You need to find product/channel fit.

Generating product/channel fit is relevant when you have developed your first product or service and look for a channel to use to access your key target customers. But it remains relevant throughout the lifecycle of your company. You will have numerous discussions with your board of directors about the performance of your channels, the potential to add further channels in order to accelerate growth, and the need to switch channels if your key target customer preferences change, and if they congregate at other places.

We discuss how to generate and measure product/channel fit in Chapter 5.

9   Traction – How Any Startup Can Achieve Explosive Customer Growth / by Gabriel Weinberg and Justin Mares.

10   Zero To One – Notes On Startups, Or How To Build The Future / by Peter Thiel.

Developing Strong Unit Economics

If you scale your business on strong unit economics, you accelerate growth after the fundamental elements of your business model have been validated. You experience high customer lifetime value, reasonably low customer acquisition costs, and a short payback period.

Given the significant importance of strong unit economics, let us quickly recap the unit economics concept and understand the underlying variables.

The customer lifetime value reflects the value you receive from a customer over the customer's lifetime with your company. In order to calculate the customer lifetime value, you add up all contributions from a customer over the customer's lifetime.

The customer acquisition costs are the total costs you incur in order to acquire a customer. You add up all marketing and sales costs you incur in a specific period of time and divide the sum by the number of new customers acquired.

Strong unit economics mean that your customer lifetime value to customer acquisition costs ratio is strong. 'Strong' is certainly relative. Your unit economics potential depends on a variety of factors like your target market, your target customers, and the business model you pursue. For instance, as a rule of thumb, investors look for software-as-a-service (SaaS) businesses with a customer lifetime value to customer acquisition costs ratio of at least three.

The payback period tells you the time it takes until you have recouped your customer acquisition costs. The payback period is important as it weighs heavily on your external cash need and growth potential. The shorter the payback period the earlier you can reinvest the money into acquiring more new customers.

If you experience strong unit economics and short payback periods you are well-positioned to accelerate growth. You acquire customers profitably and recoup your customer acquisition costs quickly. This translates into higher profitable growth and less external financing need. Smart.

In contrast, if you fuel your growth engine on weak unit economics, you usually burn through a great deal of cash and need to raise additional capital over and over again. You may constantly fuel the growth engine without ever being able to demonstrate a viable business model. This is what happened when Webvan scaled prematurely.

Webvan was a grocery home delivery company. The value proposition was the convenient delivery of high-quality grocery products at attractive price points. This was a great value proposition, wasn't it? Good prices, high quality products and great convenience. The problem was not the value proposition. The problem was that the unit economics did not work. The food retail business was already characterized by low margins. On this basis, Webvan wanted to conveniently deliver – using its own costly delivery infrastructure - high quality products at low prices. Low prices, low margins, and on top, high delivery costs. The contribution margin per customer was just insufficient in light of the costs Webvan incurred to acquire customers. The unit economics were far from strong. Before Webvan could get the unit economics right, the dot.com bubble burst and Webvan filed for bankruptcy. Allegedly, the company raised more than $800 million and is still remembered as a great example of a company that scaled prematurely on the basis of weak unit economics.

There are other companies that have been able to raise immense amounts of money in order to fuel unprofitable growth. Many food and grocery delivery companies, ride sharing companies, and e-scooter companies face unit economics issues. Some even lose money on each transaction. These companies have found investors willing to back their aggressive growth strategies because market forces require these companies to pursue a premature scaling strategy. Investors seem to believe these companies can turn their businesses profitable at some point in time. But only time will tell whether they actually can or have chronic unit economics problems.

Strong unit economics are a solid growth readiness indicator. We look deeper into the unit economics topic in Chapter 6.

Establishing a Scalable Technology

You should succeed or fail based on the viability of your business model. You should excel if you have generated product/market fit and product/channel fit. If revenue soars, you should not eventually fail because your technology infrastructure cannot cope with the increased traffic and usage that comes with high growth.

This is why establishing a scalable technology infrastructure is one of the five building blocks characterizing a solid FastScaling foundation. In simple terms, your tech has to be able to handle ten customers, a thousand customers, and thousands of customers, if you expect to ever get to a million customers.

Take Friendster for example. Friendster was one of the first social media networks and one of the fastest growing companies in the early 2000s. It was only a question of time until Friendster was to become a multi-billion dollar company. But Friendster was not able to scale its server capacities in line with customer growth. High growth in usage and traffic eventually resulted in the Friendster services running slow or going down. Friendster's initial success ebbed away. Technical issues guided frustrated users into the arms of Friendster's competitors. One of the reasons why Friendster failed was that management had not ensured a scalable technology.

You must make tech scalability a priority from day one and keep your tech scalable at any and all times. Do not lose focus in this regard. Even the biggest companies can run into tech scalability issues. Just recently, this happened to Disney when it launched Disney+, the hub for streaming Disney products. When Disney+ went live, some customers immediately faced severe service problems. Some customers complained they could not access the service at all. Others said they could not access specific content. Those who tried to reach customer service were annoyed by long waiting times, sometimes hours, until they reached the service personnel. Highly frustrated customers twittered bad reviews, which likely discouraged other potential customers from signing up. Disney responded, stressing it had underestimated the customer demand. The customer demand for Disney+ had exceeded the Disney expectations.

Tech scalability is not a 'nice to have'. Tech scalability is a 'must have', and an important prerequisite for sustainable high growth and a massive valuation. It is therefore an indispensable FastScaling building block, which we look at in Chapter 7.

Striving for Market Leadership in a Large Market

You can only achieve sustainable high growth and build a massively valuable business if you can sell your products and services to an incredibly large number of target customers.

If your target market isn't large enough, you may be able to achieve product/market fit, product/channel fit, strong unit economics, and good initial revenue and press from early adopters and first customers. But your investments in sales and marketing will not continue to yield the expected returns in terms of a continuous stream of new customers. Your growth will ebb away. You may think this is pretty basic and clear. But think again. Nine out of ten startups fail. Many fail because the founders overestimate the number of customers they can serve.

Market sizing, like ensuring tech scalability, is something that will constantly accompany you on your high growth journey. You will have to conduct a proper market sizing not only when you start out, but also when you want to launch new products, enter new markets or market segments, and if customer preferences shift.

In fact, if it comes to sizing the market, many founders jump too fast to the conclusion their target market is large enough, while it actually is not. I see too many pitch decks and board presentations in which the founders present huge bubbles with huge numbers and statements according to which the market is incredibly large. Often, subsequent discussions reveal the founders have only scratched the surface and have not conducted a proper market analysis.

Be sure your target market is as big as you think it is before you accelerate growth.

We will discuss, in Chapter 8, how to accurately size your target market. You need to be diligent in this regard. Considering market dynamics and competitive developments, you must thoroughly analyze the total addressable market (TAM), the serviceable addressable market (SAM), and the serviceable obtainable market (SOM). If you are overly optimistic, you may end up with growth that significantly slows down after you have generated initial excitement and then constantly increasing customer acquisition costs.

• • • • •

If you have established the FastScaling foundation, you can FastScale. The next chapter will provide you with an overview of why and how to FastScale.

Key Founder Takeaways

☐ The FastScaling foundation is established if five FastScaling building blocks are in place: product/market fit, product/channel fit, a scalable technology infrastructure, a large market, and strong unit economics.

☐ Product/market fit has been achieved if your products or services solve a significant customer problem and satisfy a market need.

☐ Getting to product/market fit is so important because if your products and services do not solve a significant customer problem, the customers will not buy your products. If you convince them to buy anyway, they are likely to churn fast and never return. Even worse, if they are completely dissatisfied, they may leave bad reviews that will prevent other customers from buying.

☐ You must also find a distribution channel that allows you to constantly and predictably sell your products and services on attractive economic terms. You need to find product/channel fit, too.

☐ If you have found product/market fit and product/channel fit, the viability of your business model is usually reflected in strong unit economics.

☐ Tech scalability is not a 'nice to have', it is a 'must have'. You should not eventually fail because your technology infrastructure cannot cope with the increased traffic and usage that comes with long periods of high growth. Make tech scalability a priority from day one and keep focusing on ensuring tech scalability.

☐ If it comes to sizing the market, many founders jump too fast to the conclusion their target market is large enough, while it actually is not. FastScaling requires you to be thorough in this regard.

CHAPTER 3

FastScaling

At some point there is a shift from being a product focused company to a company that is about distribution.[11]

ELAD GILL, INVESTOR AND AUTHOR OF THE 'HIGH
GROWTH HANDBOOK'

I f you have established the FastScaling foundation, you have validated the fundamental elements of your business model. You have found product/market fit and a channel through which you can sell your products on attractive economic terms. Your technology is stable, secure, and scalable, and you are looking at a large market. Strong unit economics confirm that you are ready to fuel the growth engine.

If these five FastScaling foundation building blocks are in place, you can FastScale. FastScaling consists of four FastScaling building blocks: Focusing on customer success, growing predictably, growing efficiently, and leading growth.

Focusing on Customer Success

If you want to create a sustainable, high growth business, do not

High Growth Handbook: Scaling Startups From 10 to 10,000 People / by Elad Gil.

just concentrate on generating top line growth. You do not grow sustainably if you just increase your marketing and sales spend. Your customers' expectations and preferences are constantly shifting. You constantly need to adapt your business accordingly.

Customer success must be your north star if you want to become and remain successful. If you make your customers successful, the rest will follow magically.

Your customers do not buy your products and services, or transact on your marketplace or platform, in order to increase your revenue and make *you* successful. They do so because they have a certain expectation as to what *they* can get from it. They expect that you make *them* successful. They expect a certain return on investment. In a B2B environment, this can mean that your customers expect a specific business benefit such as increased marketing or sales efficiency, a cost reduction, or a technological advancement. In a B2C environment, this may even include intangible and social benefits like fun.

*FastScaling - On the basis of **a relentless and company-wide focus on customer success**, product/market-fit, product/channel-fit, strong unit economics, and a scalable technology infrastructure, **efficiently** and **predictably leading** and **scaling** a business fast towards market leadership in a large market.*

In addition to a strong return on investment, your customers expect a great customer experience. The easier and more convenient it is for them to achieve their expected return on investment, the better the customer experience. If your customers predominantly work mobile, it is certainly inconvenient if you provide only a desktop solution. If you provide a software-as-a-service (SaaS) solution but your technology is poor and leads to bugs and slow website performance, your customers will get annoyed. Bad customer experience. Goodbye customers.

Customer success means your customers get a strong return on their investment (RoI) and have a great customer experience. This is what you should strive to achieve.

If you strive for customer success, you will grow sustainably and even faster, because customer success ultimately positively impacts your unit economics.

Customer lifetime value can be deconstructed into the revenue a customer generates, your contribution margin, and the lifetime of your customers. Customer success positively impacts all three variables. If your customers experience a great return on investment, they may be inclined to buy more of your products and services. Up- and cross-sells will increase revenue and - if you can sell higher margin products and services - your contribution margin. If you make your customers wildly successful, they will be less inclined to look at competitive products or to terminate the relationship with your company. Less churn, higher retention, and higher customer lifetime value will be the positive consequences.

But it is not only the customer lifetime value that you can significantly improve, if you focus on customer success. A focus on customer success will also lead to lower customer acquisition costs. Remember, your customer acquisition costs are determined by the marketing and sales costs you need to incur in order to acquire a customer. If your customers are immensely successful, you will experience less bad product reviews and customers will speak positively about your company and products. This will lead to a stronger brand, a higher brand recognition, and to more efficient marketing and sales activities. You may be able to generate higher quality leads and convert more of your leads to customers. Your customers may refer your products and services to other customers, which will again lead to lower costs per lead and ultimately lower customer acquisition costs. A virtuous circle.

Eventually, a higher customer contribution and lower customer acquisition costs will also reduce the time you need to recoup your customer acquisition costs. Shorter payback period. Less external financing need. Less dilution.

I have seen many founders that wanted to achieve high growth by focusing relentlessly on top line growth. Revenue, revenue, revenue. They forgot that customer needs and preferences are moving targets and companies need to constantly adapt in order to meet their customers' expectations. I always remind founders they need to focus on customer success instead. Revenue will follow. There is an invisible hand connecting customer success with high growth.

If you have achieved high growth readiness, do not focus solely on top line growth. You do not generate a sustainable high growth business by simply adding more and more marketing and sales resources. Your north star should be customer success. If your customers are successful, your unit economics will reflect this. You will acquire new customers more easily and your customer base will churn less. Less headwind in terms of bad reviews and churn and more tailwind in terms of up- and cross-sells, customer referrals, and higher conversion rates. A stronger customer base and more new customers who become advocates of your products and services. Higher growth and less cash required to fuel further growth.

Businesses that focus relentlessly on generating customer success eventually grow faster and more sustainably than companies that focus solely on revenue growth.

In Chapter 9, we explore how you can make your customers incredibly successful.

Growing Predictably

You do not impress investors if you close a big deal every once in a while. It is predictability and your ability to create a constantly running growth engine that impress them.

I usually meet founders well in advance, before they are ready for growth capital. The multiple personal touch points are good for founders and for me, as well, as the potential growth capital investor. The founders get to know me personally and how I can possibly help them grow their businesses. All meetings and calls help me as well. I understand how the founders deal with problems they need to overcome and how they think about growth. Are they only thinking about top line growth or are they on a journey to building a massively valuable business cash efficiently? I keep track of our discussions. If founders tell me they are currently at x million in revenue and will reach y million in revenue in six months' time, I follow up. If they hit their target, I am impressed, lean in, and listen. They are credible. If not, I try to help solve the issue and keep track of how they go about it. Founders need to be persistent and resilient.

Predictable revenue certainly entails many more tangible benefits. If you know how much you need to invest in order to achieve a specific revenue target, you can also predict your costs, EBITDA, and cash burn to a good extent. You do not raise more money than you actually need. Less dilution.

Getting to predictable revenue starts with predictions as to how the future may unfold. Given that uncertainty and incomplete information render impossible making right or wrong decisions, it is paramount you focus on creating and implementing a stellar planning process. The process is more important than the result. If you create and implement a proper process but miss your targets, you cannot blame yourself for having made a mistake.

A very simplified software-as-a-service (SaaS) revenue prediction example: Your customers generate on average $1,000 in monthly recurring revenue (MRR), and you want to grow your business by $1,000,000 in monthly recurring revenue. Disregarding churn for the sake of simplicity, you need to acquire 1,000 new customers in order to achieve your goal. Now, you need to analyze your conversion funnel. We assume that your target market is large enough. We further assume that you pursue an inbound marketing and inbound sales approach and convert 1% of your website visitors into customers. From there, you can calculate backwards how many website visitors your marketing team needs to generate. It needs to generate 100,000 website visitors (1,000 new customers/1% conversion rate). 100,000 website visitors turn into 1,000 customers that generate $1,000,000 in new business (1,000 new customers * $1,000 in monthly recurring revenue). On this basis, you can also calculate how you need to staff your marketing, sales, and customer success teams in order to deliver on this plan. Hiring, training, and ramp-up times need to be considered. If you know your customer acquisition costs, the customer lifetime value, and your payback period, you can also calculate what your growth predictions entail in terms of cash need.

In reality, the process is certainly more complex. You may be targeting different customer groups and using different channels. You may also be active in many geographies. And you cannot predict EBITDA and cash flow if you disregard all other departments. Other departments will have to grow, too, in order to create customer success and ultimately the revenue you want to achieve. The engineering department, the product team, and the finance team will have to grow as well. Your overhead and G&A costs will be impacted by growth. For all departments, you will have to analyze historic data and make reasonable assumptions about the future.

Predictability is the result of a thorough process in terms of analyzing what resources you need in order to predictably add revenue and achieve the revenue, EBITDA, and cash flow targets you set for yourself.

We discuss how to generate predictable revenue and run a proper forecasting process in Chapter 10.

Growing Efficiently

High predictable growth. Great! But as the subtitle of this book emphasizes, FastScaling is not only about generating high growth and building massively valuable businesses. FastScaling is also about pursuing a *smart* path to building a massively valuable business. FastScaling enables you to achieve both high growth and a massive valuation with less founder dilution on the way.

Founder dilution occurs when your company raises capital and issues new shares to investors.[12] Your own shareholding in your company is reduced, at least percentage-wise. If you own 100% of the shares in your company and raise $10 million on a $40 million pre-money valuation, your post-money valuation will be $50 million. The new investor will own 20% of the shares in your company ($10 million/$50 million) and you own the remaining 80%. Dilution!

Accelerating growth after having established the FastScaling foundation already leads to more efficient growth and less cash need. Focusing on customer success and running a diligent revenue, cost, and cash flow prediction process will positively impact your cash need. You already scale more efficiently than companies pursuing more aggressive approaches to growth.

But you can do even better if you also avoid some typical mistakes founders make, especially after they have raised growth capital. Some founders overspend on customer acquisition and do

---

12   And if you grant phantom stocks, any form of employee stock options, or any
      sort of warrants.

not find the right balance between growth and cash burn, hire too many employees too fast, or create unnecessary complexity that eventually leads to inefficient growth. Complexity is a growth killer.

We look at these patterns in more depth in Chapter 11. We also discuss how you can measure your growth efficiency.

Leading Growth

As your business develops towards a high growth company, you continually encounter new obstacles that you have to overcome.

You have to successfully lead the organization through uncertainty and many periods of change. You have to hire and say goodbye to many good employees. And you need to constantly adapt your organizational set-up. The flat non-hierarchical organizational set-up that worked when you started out may not fit the organizational requirements of a professional company with hundreds or thousands of employees and active in several international markets.

You are the founder and maybe the Chief Executive Officer (CEO). But these are only titles. Titles may make you a manager. But you need to be more than a manager if you want to orchestrate a high growth organization. You need to be a true leader!

In Chapter 12, we look at some leadership skills that you may already have or want to acquire. Strong communication skills, self-regulation, and self-awareness may help you successfully lead your organization. We also explore the importance of setting clear goals and discuss how you can achieve them. I meet many founders with great visions. Very often, it is execution that differentiates the great from the good. Execution is key.

But you are not alone. You can create a successful growth organization with strong people who help you on your way. We discuss how to build a successful high growth organization in Chapter 13. More important than a specific organizational set-up is who you attract, hire, and retain. The right people will tell you 'what' and 'how'.

In Chapter 14, we see that a high-functioning board of directors can assist you in making material operational, strategic, or financial decisions and explore how to create a high-functioning board of directors.

As a growth leader, you also have to convince investors to invest in your company and provide the cash you need to grow your business. How to raise growth capital is the topic of Chapter 15.

And then, in Chapter 16, we look at how you can prepare and successfully implement the sale of your company. The exit!

• • • • •

So far, we have discussed *why* FastScaling is a smart growth strategy and that it can be broken down into two distinct growth phases: establishing the FastScaling foundation and FastScaling. Let us now turn to the *how* and dive deeper into each of the FastScaling building blocks.

While you may be keen on directly jumping to the FastScaling chapters dealing with how you can accelerate growth and achieve predictable and efficient growth, I encourage you not to skip any of the chapters concerning the establishment of the FastScaling foundation. The FastScaling foundation building blocks need to be in place throughout your growth journey. Product/market fit, product/channel fit, unit economics, tech scalability, and market sizing are topics you will discuss on an ongoing basis with your board of directors.

Let us therefore turn to the next chapter in which we discuss how to generate and measure product/market fit, a topic that is relevant when you start a venture, expand internationally, penetrate new market segments, target new customer segments, and consider rolling out new products and product features.

Key Founder Takeaways

☐ FastScaling consists of four FastScaling building blocks: Focusing on customer success, growing predictably, growing efficiently, and leading growth.

☐ If you want to create a sustainable high growth business, do not only concentrate on generating top line growth. You do not grow sustainably if you just increase your marketing and sales spend. Your customers' expectations and preferences are constantly shifting. You need to adapt your business accordingly. Customer success needs to be your north star if you want to become and remain successful yourself.

☐ Customer success means that your customers get a strong return on their investment and have a great customer experience. This is what you should strive to achieve.

☐ If you strive for customer success, you will grow sustainably and even faster, because customer success ultimately positively impacts your unit economics. Higher customer lifetime value, lower customer acquisition costs, and shorter payback period.

☐ You do not impress investors if you close a big deal every once in a while. It is predictability and your ability to create a constantly running growth engine that impress them.

☐ Getting to predictable revenue starts with predictions as to how the future may unfold. Given that uncertainty and incomplete information render impossible making right or wrong decisions, it is paramount you focus on creating and implementing a stellar planning process. The process is more important than the result.

☐ Accelerating growth after having established the FastScaling foundation already leads to more efficient growth. You already scale more efficiently than companies pursuing more aggressive approaches to growth. But you can do even better if you also avoid some typical growth efficiency pitfalls like overspending on customer acquisition, not finding the right balance between growth and cash burn, hiring too many employees too fast, or creating unnecessary complexity.

☐ You need to be more than a manager if you want to orchestrate a high growth organization. You need to be a true leader!

☐ Strong leadership skills, great hires and a high-functioning board of directors help you successfully navigate your growth journey.

Establishing the FastScaling Foundation

CHAPTER 4

Generating Product/ Market Fit

You should measure your product/market fit as soon as possible because it will significantly impact how you operate your start-up. If you haven't reached product/market fit yet it is critical to keep your burn low and focus all resources on improving the percentage of users that say they would be very disappointed without your product. Avoid bringing in VPs of Marketing and Sales to try to solve the problem. They will only add to your burn and likely won't be any better than you at solving the problem. Instead, you (the founders) should engage existing and target users to learn how to make your product a 'must have'.[13]

SEAN ELLIS, AUTHOR OF 'HACKING GROWTH'

B uilding the FastScaling foundation starts with a laser-like focus on generating product/market fit.

Product/market fit has been achieved if your products or services solve a significant customer problem and satisfy a market need.

13   The Startup Pyramid / by Sean Ellis. Retrieved from: https://www.startup-marketing.com/the-startup-pyramid/.

Getting to product/market fit implies not only the development and improvement of your products and product features until they solve your customers' significant problems. You also have to figure out how to assess when they actually do it. Let us take a closer look at these two steps you must take in order to establish the first FastScaling building block, generating and measuring product/market fit.

Generating Product/Market Fit

Way too many founders start their businesses with an idea for products they believe people might like. They invest time and effort into developing these products. When the products have eventually been developed – sometimes after months or even years – they reach out to potential customers, only to realize their products actually do not solve a significant problem. They have wasted time and money on developing products nobody needs.

Never start with the product! Your chances to create a successful company are significantly better if you start with the market and identify a need in the market in the sense of a significant problem people have. Then develop a solution to the problem.

At the same time, it is not only early-stage companies that need to generate product/market fit. Product/market fit is a topic relevant at any stage in the lifecycle of a company. It will accompany you from the time you have started a company all the way up until you make an exit. It is relevant when you want to expand your product and service offerings, target additional customer segments, or enter new geographies. You need to generate product/market fit in all these situations before you accelerate growth. At any time, you will need to ensure that your products solve the problems of your key target customers.

This is why generating product/market fit starts with determining your key target customers and their major pain points. While many people may have the problem your products could solve, the problem may not be significant to all of them, or significant enough to all of them. You need to identify and define those for whom the problem is significant and for whom your products are a real pain killer. These are your key target customers.

FastScaling - **On the basis of** a relentless and company-wide focus on customer success, **product/ market-fit**, product/ channel-fit, strong unit economics, and a scalable technology infrastructure, efficiently and predictably leading and scaling a business fast towards market leadership in a large market.

Gather as much information as possible about your ideal customer. You want to understand clearly everything about her. Every last thing. Who is she? What are her pain points exactly? What are the challenges she faces? How does she currently deal with the problem? What kind of alternative solutions to the problems would she consider? Are these competitive solutions already available? What are the shortcomings of these competitive solutions? How much would she be willing to pay for your solution? The list goes on.

Access any publicly available data such as market research reports. Talk to your potential buyers. Conduct both online surveys and personal interviews. Continuously engage with your product, tech, marketing, sales, and customer success teams. They should be in touch with your customers and constantly gathering feedback. How are customers using your product? Which leads convert nicely into paying customers? What feedback do people give who decide not to buy? Under what circumstances would they buy? What do you have to change from a product or tech perspective? Why do people churn or do not return?

You really want to gather all the information you possibly can in order to understand the person you want to delight. You want to understand the person you are dealing with, the pain she has, and the solution she needs.

If you are sufficiently educated in this regard, you can build your products and constantly refine them. I strongly encourage you to apply the lean startup methodology and go through the 'build – measure – learn feedback loop' fast.[14] Build the product or product feature. Test an early version of it – the so called minimum viable product (MVP). Measure the outcome and gather feedback. Learn from it, so you can adjust, test, measure, and learn again until you have developed a product that solves a significant problem of your key target customers better than potentially competitive products; if possible, ten times better.

Customer feedback and how to deal with it is a topic that repeatedly pops up in board meetings. Not every feedback needs

---

14   You can learn more about the lean startup methodology here: http://theleanstartup.com.

to be translated into a new product or product features. While I encourage founders to embrace any feedback they get from their users and customers, I always request they take it with a grain of salt. Every development effort must ultimately lead to a strong return on investment, either because you get closer to product/ market fit, or because you make your key target customers more successful. And there is a pretty high probability that you will not achieve this by meeting all customer requests. There are two common mistakes I have seen founders make.

Firstly, they develop ever more product features that have been requested by customers, without analyzing the potential business impact the respective developments will have. More features do not necessarily translate into a higher willingness to pay for them. And it may not even mean that your customers are more satisfied. While some customers may desire the respective features, others may dislike the increased product complexity that comes with more features. And the more features you develop, the more complex your business gets, too. You lose focus! Remember what Steve Jobs famously said: "People think focus means saying yes to the thing you've got to focus on. But that's not what it means at all. It means saying no to the hundred other good ideas that there are. You have to pick carefully. I'm actually as proud of the things we haven't done as the things I have done. Innovation is saying no to 1,000 things."[15] Do not lose focus!

Secondly, they develop features also in order to please non-

---

15   Steve Job's Advice on the Only 4 Times You Should Say No Is Brilliant / by Marcel Schwantes. Retrieved from: https://www.inc.com/marcel-schwantes/first-90-days-steve-jobs-advice-on-the-only-4-times-you-should-say-no.html.

core target customers. Do not do this. If you try to meet the needs and requests of non-core target customers, you invest money in order to please customers who may never be really satisfied with your products and services (low willingness to pay!), who may reach out to your customer success and customer support teams over and over again (high cost!), and who may churn fast (low customer lifetime!). You need to focus on your key target customers and develop products and product features for them. You need to generate product/market fit in this specific market segment, your key target customers.

Now, if we assume the feedback you get from your key target customers gets better and better, how can you know that you have actually achieved product/market fit?

Measuring Product/Market Fit

In his Stanford University blog post, Marc Andreessen also touched upon the topic of how to measure product/market fit.[16] In this post, he said: "You can always feel when product/market fit isn't happening. The customers aren't quite getting value from the product, word of mouth isn't spreading, usage isn't growing that fast, press reviews are kind of 'blah', the sales cycle takes too long, and lots of deals never close. And you can always feel product/market fit when it is happening. The customers are buying the product just as fast as you can make it — or usage is growing just as

16   Marc Andreessen: Product/Market Fit: https://web.stanford.edu/class/ee204/ProductMarketFit.html.

fast as you can add more servers. Money from customers is piling up in your company checking account. You're hiring sales and customer support staff as fast as you can. Reporters are calling because they've heard about your hot new thing and they want to talk to you about it. You start getting entrepreneur of the year awards from Harvard Business School. Investment bankers are staking out your house. You could eat free for a year at Buck's."

Unfortunately, product/market fit is not binary. There is no one point in time everybody agrees that a company has found product/market fit. Neither a certain net promoter score, a specific ratio between customer lifetime value to customer acquisition costs, nor a certain increase in product usage can be considered conclusive in this regard. Product/market fit is rather a spectrum from obviously not yet found, through weak, all the way to strong and very strong.

As there is no clear answer to the question whether a company has found product/market fit, I encourage founders to look at all metrics that can help them make an educated decision in this regard.

There are company-centric and customer-centric metrics you can analyze.

Company-Centric Metrics

As to company-centric metrics, you may first look at the development of your unit economics.

The better your products solve your customers' problems, the better your customer lifetime value should get. Better product offerings usually translate into a higher willingness to pay, potentially better margins, and ultimately higher customer contributions. As you delight your customers, they have no reason to turn to your competitors. You can better retain your customers, which will be reflected in a longer customer lifetime. Higher customer contributions over a longer period of time will positively impact your customer lifetime value.

When measuring product/market fit in light of the development of your customer lifetime value, you may especially focus on analyzing your churn and retention rates. Look at your retention cohorts. If you are moving into the right direction towards product/market fit, each new cohort of customers should show a retention rate better than the previous cohort.

Getting closer to product/market fit will also be reflected in a positive development of your customer acquisition costs. If you successfully solve your customers' problems, your customers will talk positively about your products and services. Consequently, you will be able to attract more potential customers. The rate at which you convert potential customers into paying customers (the conversion rate) should also improve. You will have to spend less on acquiring customers; your customer acquisition costs decrease.

If you want to understand whether you have found product/market fit or are moving in the right direction, track the development of your unit economics. Be precise and look into each and every variable underlying customer lifetime value and customer acquisition costs. Analyze how these metrics develop over time. Also figure out whether you can link significant improvements to product and product feature developments or improvements. You want to understand what brings you closer to product/market fit.

Customer-Centric Metrics

But as you want to delight your customers and solve your customers' significant problems, you must put strong emphasis also on measuring customer-centric metrics.

The Net Promoter Score (NPS)

The net promoter score (NPS) is probably the most widespread customer-centric metric founders use.

Let us quickly recap how the net promoter score is being measured, before we look at some common mistakes some founders make when using the net promoter score in order to measure product/market fit.

To measure the net promoter score, you ask your customers the question: "How likely are you to recommend us to a friend or colleague?" Customers can answer on a scale from 1 to 10, with 1 being the least likely to recommend and 10 being the most. On the basis of their respective answers, you allocate your customers to three categories: detractors (0-6), passives (7-8), and promoters (9-10). You calculate the net promoter score subtracting the percentage of detractors from the percentage of promoters. As a rule of thumb, you can say that a decent net promoter score is between 25 and 50, a strong net promoter score greater than 50, and a stellar net promoter score greater than 70.

It is a good sign if your net promoter score is moving upwards continuously and if you can link jumps in the score to product developments or improvements. But the net promoter score is eventually only a number. From that number you cannot infer what kind of further product developments and improvements are required. I therefore highly recommend you supplement the net promoter score survey with follow-up qualitative questions. For instance, you could ask your passives what you have to improve in order for them to recommend your products and services.

The timing and touchpoint at which you ask for qualitative feedback plays an important role in this respect. If you want to gather information on a transactional basis to learn about your customer's opinion regarding a specific business transaction, you need to send the survey shortly after the specific transaction has occurred. For example, if you want to gather feedback on the quality of your customer onboarding process, you better ask directly after your customer has been onboarded. If you are looking for relational feedback in terms of whether the product solves your customer's problem, provides a great customer experience, and a strong return on investment, you better ask for feedback after your customer has truly experienced your product. In any case, you should ask for qualitative feedback that allows you to further adjust your products and services. Build, measure, learn.

I have seen founders who intentionally game the system to engineer a higher net promoter score. They have encouraged customers to give a higher score, cherry-picked the customers they asked, strategically timed the survey, and compensated customers for giving higher scores. The list goes on. "Please fill out the survey, but only if you give us a 9 or 10," is just one example for how you can artificially inflate the results. Even visual cues like highlighting the 9 and the 10 can have an impact on the net promoter score.

Artificially inflating the net promoter score results in wrong and biased data, jeopardizes your credibility *vis-à-vis* investors, and essentially leads to a false sense of achievement in respect of product/market fit. Be honest with yourself. Measure the net promoter score as objectively as possible.

Many founders work with the net promoter score in order to assess product/market fit for many good reasons. Customers are often more willing to answer quick surveys rather than jump on long feedback calls or to fill out extensive forms. The net promoter score is simple to calculate and it produces a number that can be tracked. And additional qualitative follow-up questions allow them to analyze why customers are actually dissatisfied.

While the net promoter score methodology has its merits, you may be able to gather strong insights from other measures, too.

Customer Referrals

Instead of asking your customers to rate the likelihood of a hypothetical future action in terms of whether they would recommend your products, you can also ask them about past actual behavior in terms of referrals. Have they actually recommended your products or services in the last six weeks? You may additionally ask your new customers whether they have purchased your products or services based on a referral.

If your chain of actual referrals is constantly increasing, you can infer that you are getting closer to product/market fit.

Analyzing actual referrals in addition to measuring the net promoter score can also help you identify if your customers say they would refer your products and services, but actually rarely do so. As actual referrals entail lower lead costs and thus lower customer acquisition costs, tracking actual referrals can facilitate understanding where an improvement in customer acquisition costs is being created.

Tracking actual referrals can be very insightful, either instead of or in addition to measuring the net promoter score.

The Customer Health Score (CHS)

The customer health score (CHS) is a metric that indicates the long-term prospect for a customer to churn or, in contrast, to become a high-value customer prone to up- and cross-sell.

Companies gather multiple dimensions of customer data, usually with a strong focus on usage and engagement, in order to establish the customer health score. Data for customer health is often visualized by using a traffic-light model, in which green stands for a healthy customer, yellow for a customer who has not yet experienced full customer success, and red for a customer who may churn and requires immediate attention. Sometimes the customer health score is also reflected in a number on a scale between 1 and 100.

The main advantage of a customer health score, especially over the net promoter score, is that it can be updated in real-time across all customers, not just a select few who answer a net promoter score survey.

The customer health score can be used as one additional indicator for product/market fit. If the majority of your customers are on red or yellow, you have a huge problem! You have not yet found product/market fit. If your customer base develops into a customer base being mainly on green and yellow, you might be on track.

The Product Stickiness Test

Rahul Vohra, the founder and CEO of Superhuman, wrote a great article about how Superhuman got to product/market fit.[17] He has been successful asking his customers how disappointed they would be if they could no longer use his service. Customers could answer 'very disappointed', 'somewhat disappointed', and 'not disappointed'. He then measured the percentage who answered, 'very disappointed'. He assumed that he had found product/market fit if 40% responded that they were 'very disappointed'. He took the 40% from Sean Ellis who found out that this was some kind of magic number. Companies that could not find product/market fit almost always had less than 40% of customers who responded,

17   How Superhuman Built an Engine to Find Product/Market fit / by Rahul Vohra. Retrieved from: https://firstround.com/review/how-superhuman-built-an-engine-to-find-product-market-fit/.

'very disappointed', whereas companies that gained strong traction exceeded 40%.[18]

It worked for Superhuman and this product stickiness test can indeed help you measure product/market fit. If nobody misses your products and services, you can question whether you have found product/market fit. You will still have to figure out whether 40% is the right number for you. But at least this number can work as a starting point and a rule of thumb. More important than the number will be the development that you can see. The more customers who respond, 'very disappointed', the closer you get to product/market fit.

The product stickiness test can also help you further improve your customer segmentation. Ask yourself if the customers who answer, 'not disappointed' will ever respond 'very disappointed'. If not, look for patterns in these customers and refine your key target customer characteristics by disregarding the customers you may never really satisfy. According to Rahul Vohra, this also worked for Superhuman: "This batch of not disappointed users should not impact your product strategy in any way. They'll request distracting features, present ill-fitting use cases, and probably be very vocal, all before they churn out and leave you with a mangled, muddled roadmap. As surprising or painful as it may seem, don't act on their feedback — it will lead you astray on your quest for product/market fit."[19]

18   The Startup Pyramid / by Sean Ellis. Retrieved from: https://www.startup-marketing.com/category/productmarket-fit/.

19   How Superhuman Built an Engine to Find Product/Market fit / by Rahul Vohra. Retrieved from: https://firstround.com/review/ how-superhuman-built-an-engine-to-find-product-market-fit/

Using Your Intuition

As product/market fit is not binary, all metrics and methods can only give you an indication as to whether you have found product/market fit. You will also have to use your intuition in this regard. Given the importance of generating product/market fit throughout the lifecycle of a company, I strongly encourage you to use as many metrics as you deem useful.

If you conclude you have not yet found product/market fit, continue focusing on generating product/market fit. Mark Andreessen, the co-founder and general partner of Andreessen Horowitz wrote in his Stanford University blog post: "When you are before product/market fit, focus obsessively on getting to product/market fit. Do whatever is required to get to product/market fit. Including changing out people, rewriting your product, moving into a different market, telling customers no when you don't want to, telling customers yes when you don't want to, raising that fourth round of highly dilutive venture capital — whatever is required."[20]

There is no short cut. The founders who believe there is a short cut are the ones who usually scale prematurely and fail. Do not make this mistake. Do whatever you can to generate product/market fit first.

If you believe you have found product/market fit, do not fall into the trap of assuming that you will never lose it. Your custom-

20   Product/Market Fit / by Marc Andreessen. Retrieved from: https://web. stanford.edu/class/ee204/ProductMarketFit.html.

er's needs and preferences change, and they change quickly and regularly. Constantly track relevant metrics. And plan to adapt.

● ● ● ● ●

Having found product/market fit does not mean you are ready to fuel the growth engine. Product/market fit is important, but it is by no means all that matters. What good is product/market fit if you cannot find a distribution channel to sell your products on attractive economic terms? You will also have to find product/channel fit. We will discuss how to generate product/channel fit in the next chapter.

Key Founder Takeaways

- ☐ Building the FastScaling foundation starts with a laser-like focus on generating product/market fit.

- ☐ Product/market fit has been achieved if your products solve a significant customer problem and satisfy a market need.

- ☐ Product/market fit is a topic relevant at any stage in the lifecycle of a company. It is not only relevant when you start a business. It is of paramount importance when you want to expand your product and service offerings, target additional customer segments, or enter new geographies. You need to generate product/market fit in all these situations before you accelerate growth.

- ☐ While many people may have the problem your products could solve, the problem may not be significant to all of them. You need to identify and define your key target customers for whom the problem is significant and for whom your products are a real pain killer. You need to generate product/market fit in this market segment of key target customers.

- ☐ If you understand the exact needs and pains of your key target customers, you can go through the 'build – measure – learn feedback loop' fast and build and refine your products and product features.

☐ Make sure every product and product feature development effort translates into a strong return on investment, either because you get closer to product/market fit or because you make your key target customers more successful.

☐ Product/market fit is not binary. There is no one point in time everybody agrees that a company has found product/market fit. But you may gather and analyze both company-centric and customer-centric metrics in order to answer the question whether you have found product/market fit.

☐ Product/market fit will have a significant impact on customer lifetime value and customer acquisition costs. Track these metrics and analyze how they develop over time and whether you can link significant improvements to product and product feature developments or improvements.

☐ Many founders work with the net promoter score in order to assess product/market fit. Do not artificially inflate the net promoter score. Artificially inflating the net promoter score results in wrong and biased data, jeopardizes your credibility *vis-à-vis* investors, and essentially leads to a false sense of achievement with respect to product/market fit. Be honest with yourself. Measure the net promoter score as objectively as possible.

☐ Instead of or in addition to using the net promoter score, you may also ask your customers about past actual behavior in terms of actual referrals, track the customer health score (CHS), or use the product stickiness test.

☐ Eventually, all metrics and methods can only give you an indication as to whether you have found product/market fit. You will also have to use your intuition in this regard.

☐ If you believe you have not yet found product/market fit, do whatever is required to get to product/market fit. If you believe you have found product/market fit, do not fall into the trap of assuming that you will never lose it. Your customer's needs and preferences change. And they change quickly and regularly. Constantly track relevant metrics. And plan to adapt.

CHAPTER 5

Generating Product/ Channel Fit

Statements like 'Product/Market Fit is the only thing that matters' have become more common. It is not the only thing that matters.[21]

BRIAN BALFOUR, FOUNDER AND CEO AT REFORGE AND

FORMER VP GROWTH AT HUBSPOT

Product/market fit is necessary. You need to get to product/ market fit before you accelerate growth. But it is by no means all that matters. You also have to find product/channel fit in terms of a predictable and scalable distribution channel through which you can sell your products on attractive economic terms.

At the very start of your company, you will look for a first channel through which you can sell your products and services. But then, over time, it is also critical to keep looking for additional channels or considering switching channels.

---

21 Why Product/Market Fit Isn't Enough / by Brian Balfour. Retrieved from: https://brianbalfour.com/essays/product-market-fit-isnt-enough.

For instance, your key customer preferences may change in terms of where they congregate. If you sell to end consumers and they change their behavior and spend more and more time on a new social media platform, you may have to change your channel or add this new platform to your channel mix.

If you want to accelerate growth, your board of directors will always want to know whether you can do so by adding new channels and thereby acquiring more customers each month.

A company that is not innovative and does not come up with new innovative products on a recurring basis is doomed to fail. New innovative products may not fit your existing channels but may need to be sold through new channels. Again, you will have to look for product/channel fit.

*FastScaling - **On the basis of** a relentless and company-wide focus on customer success, product/market-fit, **product/channel-fit**, strong unit economics, and a scalable technology infrastructure, efficiently and predictably leading and scaling a business fast towards market leadership in a large market.*

Therefore, the product/channel fit topic is relevant not only at the very start of your business. Product/channel fit is a topic relevant at all stages in the lifecycle of your company. Do not be surprised if your board of directors repeatedly asks you to report on the performance of your channels and potential additional channels you may sell through.

I have just recently been involved in an exit of a portfolio company. In connection with the commercial due diligence, the acquirer wanted to understand, in detail, how the company performed in each target customer segment, in each market, in each product category, and in each channel. A strong management team has this information available with a push of a button. The numbers need to demonstrate that it makes sense from an economic perspective to grow the company in these respective markets, to sell the respective products and product features to the respective customer segments, and to distribute the products and services through the respective channels.

In light of the enduring paramount importance of distributing your products through channels on attractive economic terms, let us look at how you can generate and measure product/channel fit.

Generating Product/Channel Fit

In connection with generating product/market fit, you have already segmented your market and defined your key target customers. You know to whom you are going to sell. Generating product/channel fit builds on this exercise and deals with exploring, prioritizing, testing, and deploying potential distribution channels through which you can sell your products to your key target customers.

If you have already generated significant traction and want to expand internationally, penetrate additional customer segments, or sell new products and product features, you will also need to start with your target customers and the exact needs they have. If you have clearly defined your key target customers and their characteristics and needs, you must explore potential channels to your target audience.

Creating Cross-Functional Teams

In my experience, it helps to create cross-functional teams that brainstorm potentially relevant channels, prioritize channels, and ensure that relevant channels are being tested and deployed.

Cross-functional teams make sure your teams do not work in silos and do not come up with channels that only work from their functional expertise perspective. For instance, there is no value in using a channel that the marketing and sales teams prefer if the product and tech teams cannot adjust your product so it fits this particular channel. Likewise, you will not be able to scale a channel successfully if your product teams want to build highly complex products that your marketing and sales teams cannot distribute successfully.

Cross-functional teams look at potential channels holistically. If you want to test and deploy channels highly explored and studied, and based on input from all constituencies, involve marketing, sales, product, tech, finance, and customer success.

Exploring Distribution Channels

The whole exercise of exploring channels starts with identifying potential channels to your key target customers. At the beginning, do not disregard any channel as irrelevant, but consider all channels that come to mind. Then check whether you can get in touch with your key target customers through the channels you have determined. If you can potentially get access to your key target customers through the channels you have identified, start prioritizing them.

Prioritizing Distribution Channels

As the term 'product/channel fit' indicates, not every channel fits your products and your products do not fit every channel. When you prioritize channels, you need to identify the channels that already fit your products and those that you could use if you adjusted your products accordingly. As Brian Balfour[22], the CEO at Reforge and former VP of Growth at HubSpot, rightfully stressed: "Products are built to fit channels, not the other way around. Channels do not mold to products. The reason for this is that you do not define the rules of the channel. You define your product, but the channel defines the rules of the channel."[23] For instance, chances are high you cannot tell Facebook how the platform must adapt so you can sell your products through Facebook. But you may be able to develop your products so they can be sold through a specific channel like Facebook.

Prioritizing channels also means that you educate yourself as

---

22   You may want to check out more articles that Brian Balfour published on product/market fit and product/channel fit here: https://brianbalfour.com/essays.

23   Product Channel Fit Will Make or Break Your Growth Strategy / by Brian Balfour: Retrieved from: https://brianbalfour.com/four-fits-growth-framework.

much as possible before you deprioritize certain channels. Talk to your key target customers, potential channel owners, and channel partners, in order to get a good understanding of what each of these constituencies expects from you.

As to your key target customers, you want to understand where they spend their time. You want to know whether your key target customers expect and appreciate to be targeted there. You also want to educate yourself about what they expect at each and every touchpoint along the customer journey and especially how they like the communication to take place. Some customers may expect to purchase through no-touch or low-touch channels where they do not or only sporadically talk to anybody in person. Other customers, in contrast, may explicitly expect a high-touch acquisition and onboarding approach with human interaction. They may want personal explanations as to how the products solve their problems and look for human support in case something goes wrong; a pattern you will often see when you sell to enterprise customers.

With regard to channel partners, you need to understand why they could be interested in helping you distribute your products. They will be interested if they see significant value *for themselves* in working with you. Otherwise, they will not care at all. That's business. For example, I have seen founders who negotiated extremely hard with potential channel partners in order to get the most favorable terms for themselves. They negotiated terms that looked nice on paper for them but removed any significant incentive for the channel partners to actually help distribute the products. You need to create win-win-situations if you want to work successfully with channel partners. A channel or partner is just like a customer. You have to work for them if you expect them to work for you.

Therefore, do not only put yourself in the shoes of your key target customers but also in the shoes of your channel partners. Only if you understand and meet their interests you can be successful yourself. First the customer, then the channel partners, only then think of yourself and what you can get from it. As soon as the channel works, the rest will follow naturally.

Finding Predictable and Scalable Distribution Channels

If you want to grow fast, you must prioritize channels that enable you to scale your business predictably and sustainably over the long run. You will have to prioritize your potential channels in light of the volume of leads you can generate and whether you can constantly convert an attractive number of leads into customers. Certainly, there is a link to the size of your target market. If your target market is not large enough, you will never be able to constantly and predictably scale a channel to your customers.

Let us assume you run a B2B software-as-a-service (SaaS) company, targeting big enterprise customers. Let us further assume that your company has already achieved significant traction and can spend $500,000 per month on marketing and sales in order to generate 2,000 leads to your key target customers. Let us further assume your conversion funnel is as follows: You convert 25% of your leads into marketing qualified leads (MQL), 20% of your marketing qualified leads into sales qualified leads (SQL), and 10% of your sales qualified leads into customers. Accordingly, you end up with ten new paying customers.

Here is the math (rounded figures):

2,000 Leads * 25% = 500 Marketing Qualified Leads (MQL)

500 Marketing Qualified Leads * 20% = 100 Sales Qualified Leads (SQL)

100 Sales Qualified Leads * 10% = 10 Customers

If you want to analyze whether you can scale this channel predictably, look into the past, first. On the basis of your historic monthly investments of $500,000, have you been able to constantly generate 2,000 leads and convert them into 10 paying customers, which would translate into a 0.5% conversion rate from lead to customer (10/2,000) and customer acquisition costs of $50,000 ($500,000/10)? If you have not been constantly investing $500,000, check whether your conversion rate and customer acquisition costs have been stable.

If you have not been able to constantly achieve a certain number of leads, a stable conversion rate, or constant customer acquisition costs, you need to look into why this has not been the case and whether you can change something, so you get to a more stable number of leads and a relatively constant conversion rate. Again, as you may not be able to adapt the channel, you must look into whether you can change something product or process related.

If you have been able to constantly generate and convert your leads, you need to look ahead and predict the future. Can you comfortably argue that you can continue to generate 2,000 leads each month? If so, could you also increase the number of leads you generate if you increased your marketing spend? In this case, will the conversion rate remain the same in the sense that you can convert, for example, 10,000 leads into 50 customers? And for how long can you do so? In order to calculate the time you can continue to generate and convert a certain number of leads, you need to link your predictions to your market sizing efforts. If you have calculated that there are 1,000,000 key target customers out there in a specific target region, you could theoretically generate 10,000 leads for a period of 100 months (1,000,000/10,000).

This is only theory. In reality, leads that could not be converted initially may be touched again later on. And you may probably never be able to reach all key target customers anyway. Seasonality can also play an important role in the sense that you may be able to generate and convert leads differently in specific times during the calendar year. In addition, there is usually a deterioration in the conversion rate the longer you penetrate a specific market and the closer you get to market saturation. But on the basis of these calculations, you can get to an educated view about the attractiveness, and ultimately the predictability and scalability, of a specific channel. Prioritize predictable and scalable channels!

Testing Distribution Channels

After you have prioritized your channels, you can start testing them. You test a channel and measure its effectiveness and efficiency. How many leads can you generate, at what cost, and how do such leads convert into customers? What does the conversion funnel look like, especially compared to other channels? What are your customer acquisition costs in this channel? Also, in connection with generating product/channel fit, you go through the 'build – measure – learn feedback loop.' Learn from the results and adjust product and process so the channel performance improves.

Working in Parallel on Product/Market Fit and Product/Channel Fit

Your cross-functional teams need to work in parallel on generating product/market fit and product/channel fit, and not consecutively. Both generating product/market fit and generating product/channel fit may require your teams to adapt and adjust the product, the product features, your processes, your key target customer definition, or your team composition. You do not want to generate product/market fit just to realize that you need to adjust the product and product features again in order to be able to sell it through a specific channel. Generating product/market fit and product/channel fit go hand in hand.

Measuring Product/Channel Fit

How do you know you have found product/channel fit? As it is true with regard to measuring product/market fit, product/channel fit is not binary either.

You cannot say you have achieved product/channel fit if it costs you X dollars to acquire a customer. The absolute dollar number depends on many factors like the channel you use, but also the complexity of your product, and the characteristics of your key target customers. While spending $10,000 on acquiring an enterprise customer with a high customer lifetime value can make sense, this amount may be prohibitive if you want to sell to small business customers or consumers with a very low willingness to pay.

Product/channel fit can range from 'not yet found' through 'weak' all the way to 'very strong'. And product/channel fit is relative. You need to analyze your channels assessing whether the customer acquisition costs you incur using a specific channel make sense in light of the customer lifetime value you can extract from the customers you acquire through this specific channel. For instance, is it worth $10,000 to acquire a customer who will spend $25,000 over the next five years? We will explore this unit economics concept in more depth in the next chapter. But, in a nutshell, you need to make sure that your customer lifetime value reasonably exceeds your customer acquisition costs and that your payback period is reasonably short. If you target customers with a high customer lifetime value you may be able to use channels that lead to high customer acquisition costs, often high touch channels that require intensive human touch. If your key target customer lifetime value is rather low, you will have to use channels through which you can acquire customers in a less expensive manner, many times low-touch or no-touch channels in which digital touch replaces human touch.

During the last five years, I have looked intensively at the restaurant tech industry in order to find startups that help restaurateurs become more digital. A major problem almost all startups faced was that restaurateurs were difficult to reach and usually required a human touch when it came to convincing them to buy. Some startups tried to sell their products using a field sales force who traveled to individual restaurants to sell products and services. The costs associated with using a field sales force were certainly incredibly high and so were the customer acquisition costs. At the same time, most restaurateurs ran low margin businesses and did not yet see much value in using digital products and services. The restaurateurs' willingness to pay was therefore usually rather low. While I have seen startups that could sell their products predictably through this high-touch channel and could even successfully scale this channel by adding more and more 'feet on the street', the unit economics rarely worked. Customer acquisition costs were way too high in relation to the customer lifetime value the startups could extract from the customers acquired.

Measuring product/channel fit therefore goes hand in hand with calculating your unit economics. While you certainly always want to find ways to reduce your customer acquisition costs, you need to find and prioritize channels through which you can acquire customers on attractive economic terms, which means that your customer acquisition costs must be sufficiently lower than your customer lifetime value.

Optimizing the Conversion Funnel

As soon as you believe you have found product/channel fit, do not immediately jump to exploring the next channel. You may be surprised how much additional growth you can generate by improving your existing channel in terms of acquiring more customers with the same money spent on marketing and sales.

Let us continue with our software-as-a-service (SaaS) company example. Your company spends $500,000 per month on marketing and sales and generates 2,000 leads to your enterprise key target customers. We assumed a conversion rate of 25% from lead to marketing qualified lead (MQL), a 20% conversion rate from marketing qualified lead to sales qualified lead (SQL) and a 10% conversion rate from sales qualified lead to customer. Your company ends up generating ten customers per month.

If your company improved the conversion rate at each stage of the conversion funnel by only 10%, it could increase the number of new customers from 10 to 13.

Here is the math (rounded figures):

2,000 Leads * 27.5% = 550 Marketing Qualified Leads (MQL)

550 Marketing Qualified Leads * 22% = 121 Sales Qualified Leads (SQL)

121 Sales Qualified Leads * 11% = 13 Customers

If you could improve the conversion rate at each stage of the conversion funnel by 20%, you could increase the number of new customers from 10 to 17.

Here is the math again (again rounded figures):

2,000 Leads * 30% = 600 Marketing Qualified Leads (MQL)

600 Marketing Qualified Leads * 24% = 144 Sales Qualified Leads (SQL)

144 Sales Qualified Leads * 12% = 17 Customers

While this is certainly only theory, this example demonstrates nicely how your company could increase the number of monthly new customers significantly by optimizing the conversion funnel only slightly.

At the same time, the optimized conversion funnel would lead to significantly lower customer acquisition costs. $500,000 spent on marketing and sales leads to customer acquisition costs of $50,000 in the original example ($500,000/10 new paying customers), $38,462 in the example with a conversion rate improved by 10% ($500,000/13 new paying customers) and $29,412 in the example with a conversion rate improved by 20% ($500,000/17 new paying customers).

Since a better conversion rate leads to more paying customers, it also leads to more growth. Assuming an average monthly recurring revenue (MRR) of $2,500 per paying enterprise customer, the new monthly recurring revenue amounts to $25,000 in the original example (10 new customers * $2,500 new MRR), $32,500 in the example with a conversion rate improved by 10% (13 new customers * $2,500 new MRR), and $42,500 in the example with a conversion rate improved by 20% (17 new customers * $2,500 new MRR). Correspondingly, the new annual recurring revenue (ARR)[24] amounts to $300,000, $390,000 and $510,000 respectively.

Assuming an average customer lifetime of 48 months, a contribution margin (CM) of 80%, and the same monthly recurring revenue of $2,500 per paying customer, the customer lifetime value is $96,000 ($2,500 new MRR * 80% CM * 48 months). In the original example, the customer lifetime value to customer acquisition costs ratio is 1.92 ($96,000 CLV/$50,000 CAC). In the example in which the conversion rate is improved by 10%, the customer lifetime value to customer acquisition costs ratio is 2.5 ($96,000 CLV/$38,462 CAC). In the example in which your company found ways to improve the conversion rate by 20%, the customer lifetime value to customer acquisition costs ratio is 3.3 ($96,000 CLV/$29,412 CAC). As a rule of thumb, investors look for software-as-a-service (SaaS) companies with a customer lifetime value to customer acquisition costs ratio greater than 3.

If your company improves its conversion funnel and spends less on acquiring a customer, the payback period gets shorter, too. In the original example, it takes 25 months to pay back the customer acquisition costs (CAC of $50,000/($2,500 new MRR * 80% CM)). In the example in which the conversion rate is improved by 10%, the payback period is reduced to 20 months (CAC of

---

24   Annual recurring revenues are the monthly recurring revenues multiplied by 12.

$38,462/(\$2,500$ new MRR $*$ 80% CM)). In the example in which you find ways to improve the conversion rate by 20%, the payback period is reduced to 15 months (CAC of $29,412/(\$2,500$ new MRR $*$ 80% CM)). For your business, a reduced payback period means that the money invested to acquire a customer can be reinvested earlier again in order to acquire additional customers. Shorter payback periods lead to higher growth, less cash need, and less dilution for you as the founder!

You can accelerate growth, reduce your cash need, and create a more attractive business with a potentially higher exit valuation by optimizing the conversion funnel.

Whether and how a company can improve the conversion funnel, and at which stage of the funnel, is something that needs to be analyzed on a case-by-case basis. You should look at each step of the funnel. As a starting point, you will find below some questions you may ask your cross-functional teams:

- Do our marketing activities actually attract our key target customers? Only if you attract your key target customers, your marketing and sales teams can nurture high-quality leads that convert, with a higher probability, into successful customers. Higher conversion rate and lower customer acquisition costs.

- Do we remove leads to non-key target customers early on? Removing bad and unqualified leads early on will significantly improve your conversion rate. Your marketing and sales teams do not spend time and resources on leads with a low probability of converting into customers. Thus, they can spend even more time on converting high-quality leads. More time for preparation, more time to follow-up, and hence again higher conversion rates and lower customer acquisition costs.

- Do we have several key target customer groups and landing pages tailored to each and every target audience? Your landing pages are where your potential customers land after they have searched for relevant information and clicked on the links to your website. Your landing pages create a first impression of your company, your products and services. Your landing pages must be just great from both a relevant content perspective and a customer experience perspective. Loading times must be extremely short and the content your potential customers find on your landing pages must be absolutely relevant for them.

- Do we understand the typical buyer journey and have relevant content for our buyer personas at each and every touchpoint of the buyer journey? Remarkable content is what drives your marketing success across channels. Through creating relevant content that stands out, you build a strong brand that potential buyers trust, differentiate yourself from your competition, become search-relevant, and lay the foundation for attracting your key target customers.

- Do we pursue a sophisticated lead scoring methodology? Lead scoring is the process of assessing the quality of the leads that have gone into the conversion funnel. This process helps sales and marketing teams prioritize leads, so they can work on the most promising leads, interact with them correspondingly, and improve the overall lead to customer conversion rate. Whatever methodology your teams pursue, you must ensure that your marketing team scores the leads in a sophisticated manner based on attributes of leads that have become customers, on attributes of leads that have not become customers, feedback from your marketing, sales and customer success teams, and feedback from your customers. Your marketing team should build a model around the attributes that increase the likelihood of a lead becoming a customer. It should constantly check whether the lead scoring methodology needs to be adjusted based on new information available, new winning trends, or new marketing channels available.[25]

- Are leads passed on to the next stage of the funnel at the right time? The sales team is probably among the most expensive resources in your company. This team should only touch high-quality leads, and only if and when the respective buyer is ready and open for a dialogue with your sales team.

[25] I can recommend you read the respective chapter in: The Sales Acceleration Formula: using data, technology, and inbound selling to go from $0 to $100 million / by Mark Roberge.

- Are our product, tech, finance, marketing, sales, and customer success teams working as one team towards the common goal of establishing product/market fit and product/channel fit?

Adding Additional Growth Channels

Many founders who have managed to successfully scale and optimize one channel try to accelerate growth by adding another channel. They may have successfully pursued an inbound marketing go-to-market approach and want to add an outbound channel now. Or they have successfully scaled direct channels to their customers and now want to add indirect channels where they sell their products through resellers and other channel partners.

Based on my experience as a board member of companies who have also tried to generate product/channel fit in more than one channel, it is true that most businesses actually get zero distribution channels to work. Poor distribution — not product — is the number one cause of failure. If you can get just one distribution channel to work, you have a great business.[26]

My advice here has always been not to be over-confident. Do not invest heavily in the second channel just because you have found product/channel fit in the first channel. You have hopefully deliberately chosen the first channel over the one you are now willing to test, because the first channel was more promising... factually and statistically. And just because you can sell your products through one channel does not mean you can sell through other channels as well. It should have become clear, meanwhile, that your products need to fit not only the market but also the channel.

Does this mean that you should not explore further channels? Definitely not. If you manage to make more than one distribution channel work, you are among very few companies and on track to creating something great and extraordinary. And you must constantly explore other channels anyway. Customer behavior in terms of where customers can be found as well as their preferences and expectations change over time. New channels emerge. You may have to go through these new channels to acquire customers.

• • • • •

As you have seen, generating product/channel fit requires you to relentlessly measure customer-centric and company-centric metrics like your unit economics. This is the topic of the next chapter.

Key Founder Takeaways

☐ What good is product/market fit if you cannot find a distribution channel through which you can sell your products on attractive economic terms? You will also have to find product/channel fit.

☐ Product/channel fit is a topic relevant throughout the lifecycle of your company. At the very start of your venture, you must find a first distribution channel. If customer preferences change, you may need to adapt and switch channels. If you want to accelerate growth, you may have to add channels to the channel mix. If you want to be an innovative company, you may need to find new channels through which you can sell new products and services.

☐ Generating product/channel fit starts with creating a cross-functional team that brainstorms potentially relevant channels, prioritizes channels, and ensures that relevant channels are being tested and deployed.

☐ At the beginning, consider all channels that come to mind. If you can potentially get access to your key target customers through the channels you have identified, start prioritizing them.

☐ Prioritizing channels includes educating yourself as much as possible before you exclude certain channels. Talk to your key target customers and potential channel partners in order get a good understanding of what each of these constituencies expects from you.

☐ If you want to use indirect channels and work with channel partners, like resellers, you need to understand why they could be interested in helping you distribute your products. If channel partners do not see significant value in working with you, you are doomed to fail. First the customer, then the channel partners, only then think of yourself and what you can get from it.

☐ Prioritize channels that you can scale predictably and sustainably over the long run.

☐ After you have prioritized your channels, you can start testing them. You go through the 'build – measure – learn feedback loop' and adjust your product, product features, marketing activities and processes until the respective channel performs better and better.

☐ Your cross-functional teams should work in parallel on generating product/market fit and product/channel fit, and not consecutively. You do not want to generate product/market fit just to realize that you need to adjust the product and product features again in order to sell it through a specific channel.

☐ Product/channel fit is not binary. It can go from 'not yet found' through 'weak' all the way to 'very strong'. And product/channel fit is relative. You can measure product/channel fit assessing whether the customer acquisition costs you incur using a specific channel make sense in light of the customer lifetime value associated with the customers you acquire through this specific channel.

☐ If you target customers with a high customer lifetime value, you may be able to also use channels that lead to high customer acquisition costs. If your key target customer lifetime value is rather low, you will have to prioritize and use channels through which you can acquire customers in a less expensive manner (mostly low-touch or no-touch channels).

☐ As soon as you have found product/channel fit, focus on improving the channel by optimizing your conversion funnel. Optimizing the conversion funnel will not only lead to more customers, but also to lower customer acquisition costs, better unit economics, shorter payback periods, and ultimately higher profitable growth.

☐ Do not be over-confident when it comes to adding channels. Most startups only get one channel to work.

☐ But you must constantly explore additional channels. If you manage to make more than one distribution channel work, you are among very few
companies and on track to creating something great
and extraordinary.

CHAPTER 6

Developing Strong Unit Economics

You can create infinite revenue if you sell dollars for 85 cents. And if you give consumers more value than you charge them for, they will love you. And I remind entrepreneurs all the time that Webvan had the highest NPS scores of any company I've ever known. It wasn't that the consumer proposition didn't work, it was that the economics didn't work.[27]

BILL GURLEY, GENERAL PARTNER AT BENCHMARK

The unit economics concept is a powerful tool that helps you better understand whether you are pursuing a viable business model. Strong unit economics tell you that you make money on the units you sell and the customers you acquire. With strong unit economics, the fundamental elements of your business model have been validated.

---

27   Benchmark General Partner Bill Gurley on Recode Decode. Retrieved from: https://www.vox.com/2016/9/28/13095682/bill-gurley-benchmark-bubble-uber-recode-decode-podcast-transcript.

Unit economics describe how much value a single unit generates for your business. You compare the costs you incur with the contribution such unit generates. You can run a unit economics analysis on all sorts of units like products sold, transactions completed, a single user and a cohort of users, a single customer or a cohort of customers. All these analyses can make sense and whether or not you want to understand the unit economics for these units highly depends on your business model. The most common and most important unit economics analysis looks at a single customer.

*FastScaling - **On the basis of** a relentless and company-wide focus on customer success, product/market-fit, product/channel-fit, **strong unit economics**, and a scalable technology infrastructure, efficiently and predictably leading and scaling a business fast towards market leadership in a large market.*

The Unit Economics Concept

The customer lifetime value (CLV) reflects the value that you receive from a customer over the customer's lifetime. In order to calculate the customer lifetime value, you add up all customer contributions over the customer's lifetime. You calculate it by multiplying the revenues a customer generates per month with your contribution margin (CM) and the average customer lifetime in months.

Customer Lifetime Value (CLV) = Revenue per Customer per Month * Contribution Margin (CM) * Lifetime in Months

If you have found product/market fit, you solve a significant problem of your customers. Your customers should have a correspondingly high willingness to pay and become loyal customers who stick around. Assuming a compelling contribution margin, you experience a high customer lifetime value.

The customer acquisition costs (CAC) are the total costs you incur in order to acquire a customer. You take the total of all marketing and sales costs you incur in a specific period of time and divide it by the number of new customers acquired.

Customer Acquisition Costs (CAC) = (Marketing Costs + Sales Costs)/Number of New Customers Acquired

If you have found product/channel fit, you have found a working distribution channel through which you can sell your products and services on attractive economic terms. You experience reasonably low customer acquisition costs compared to your customer lifetime value.

The payback period informs you about the time it takes until you have recouped your customer acquisition costs. You divide your customer acquisition costs by the monthly customer contribution.

Payback Period = Customer Acquisition Costs (CAC)/(Revenue per Customer per Month * Contribution Margin (CM))

Generating Strong Unit Economics

Calculating your unit economics is not only about analyzing how you are doing. More importantly, it is about improving and steering your business in the right direction. You can create high profitable growth and steer your business fast towards a massive valuation by deconstructing the unit economics metrics into their components and improving each and every component. Let's have a look.

The customer lifetime value can be deconstructed into the revenues a customer generates, your contribution margin, and the lifetime of your customers. You can therefore improve your customer lifetime value by improving the revenues a customer generates, your contribution margin, and the lifetime of your customers.

The revenues generated by a customer in a given month can be further deconstructed into the number of transactions per customer and the price you can charge per transaction. You can improve revenues by increasing the price point and the number of transactions per customer. In essence, you want to find the perfect match between price and number of transactions, the price and quantity equilibrium. If you have reached this level, you may want to dig even deeper and understand why your customers may not be willing to pay a higher price or do not return more often to buy from your company. Maybe this is due to product performance, a lack of product features, or competition. You will have to figure it out.

You can also look more closely at your contribution margin to understand how you can reduce your costs of goods sold (CoGS) and all other variable costs per product or service sold.

As to the customer lifetime, you are interested in understanding why customers terminate contracts and churn, cannot be retained longer, or do not return. You need to understand the churn and retention issues and what you can do about them.

It certainly depends on your business, the market you are active in, and your business model, whether and how you can improve the variables underlying customer lifetime value. However, since this is a topic I regularly discuss with founders, let me share with you some of the actions that worked well.

Price increases usually work better than founders think. Founders are very often extremely reluctant to increase prices. Many founders fear that price increases prevent new customers from buying or lead to higher churn rates and lower retention rates, respectively. They believe that higher prices lead to lower growth and the other way around. This is counterintuitive if the same founders argue they have a significant competitive advantage and their products are ten times better than competitive products. Do not be too cautious in this regard. If you really have a competitive advantage, price increases can make a great deal of sense. They can improve your unit economics and provide you with additional money you can invest into fueling the growth engine even further. Higher profitable growth is very often the consequence of price increases. A smart way to increase prices is to test them first at small scale, for instance in a specific region, with a specific product or in a specific customer segment, before rolling them out.

In connection with discussing price increases you should also reflect on the pricing strategy you pursue. It is often easier to pursue a cost-plus pricing strategy by calculating your unit costs and adding a margin, or to work with a competitive pricing strategy where you set your price point based on what your competitors charge. But again, if you believe you have a competitive advantage and can win the market, you may be better off pursuing a value-based pricing strategy, even and especially if this pricing strategy leads to even higher prices. Under a value-based pricing strategy you set the price on the basis of the value you create for your customers and their corresponding willingness to pay. Value-based pricing requires you to generate a huge amount of data and information about your customers willingness to pay. At the same time, if you pursue the FastScaling strategy you will gather that data anyway in order to generate and measure product/market fit and customer success. It is worth the effort.

You can improve your customer lifetime value not only by increasing your price points, but also by reducing the direct costs that need to be considered in your contribution margin. The general advice here is twofold. Firstly, you certainly need to accurately calculate your contribution margin and look at each cost position in order to figure out which position you can improve and how. Secondly, you can explore how expensive human touch points can be avoided and replaced by digital touch points. For instance, if your business requires customer support and customer success functions responsible for ensuring the customers can use your products and services or solving customer problems, you should explore whether you can deploy digital solutions in this regard.[28]

28   If and to the extent customer success personnel is not taking care of up- and
      cross-selling, but help customers use the products and services, they should
      be considered costs of goods sold (CoGS) or other direct costs. In particular at
      software-as-a-service (SaaS) companies, customer success costs must very often
      be considered costs of goods sold (CoGS).

Digital in-product solutions and self-service videos can facilitate your activation and onboarding activities and reduce human touch points required. Digital solutions, like chat bots, can replace human first level support and reduce the customer support costs. In general, you should look across departments in order to figure out where you can reduce human touch without negatively impacting customer success. The more you create a low-touch and no-touch business model, the better your unit economics and overall company efficiency should get, as long as your customers remain highly delighted and incredibly successful.

If you want to improve your customer churn and retention rates, I encourage you to review your customer cohorts in order to analyze at what point in time your customers churn or do not return anymore. If you have identified the respective data points, you need to dive deep and analyze the reasons for this customer behavior. Your findings need to go into your product or tech roadmap.

You can improve your customer acquisition costs by generating more customers with the same amount spent on marketing and sales, or by generating the same number of customers with a smaller amount spent on marketing and sales. Improving your customer acquisition costs therefore boils down to improving your conversion funnel. In other words, improving the efficiency of your marketing and sales efforts will directly lead to lower customer acquisition costs. In the previous chapter, we have already looked at how to optimize the conversion funnel and the respective impact such improvements can have.

You can shorten your payback period by reducing your customer acquisition costs and improving your customers' contribution.

If you want to generate strong unit economics by improving the variables underlying the unit economics concept, you need to calculate them correctly in the first place. In the Appendix, you will find a detailed and relatively math-heavy description of how to correctly calculate unit economics for recurring revenues businesses, e-commerce businesses, and platform businesses. I encourage you to read at least the parts dealing with your business model.

Carefully Scrutinizing Averages

You usually calculate the unit economics using a variety of averages like the average churn rate, the average revenue per customer, or the average marketing and sales costs per customer acquired. More importantly than absolutely following the exact calculation methodologies should always be that you apply your business acumen. Numbers are great but should be tempered with common sense. Beware of working with averages. Working with averages can be meaningless and guide you in the wrong direction.

For instance, I looked at a startup that ran a software-as-a-service (SaaS) business with two distinct key target customer groups, mid-sized businesses and small businesses, and an average churn rate of 4%.[29] This churn rate was absolutely unsustainable as it

29   Approximately 50% of the customers were mid-sized businesses and 50% small businesses.

meant that the company lost its complete existing customer base on average after 25 months.[30] The unit economics calculated on the basis of an average churn rate did not work either. The high average churn rate led to a very low average customer lifetime value. However, looking into each target customer group separately revealed a different picture. While 7% of the mid-sized business customers churned each month, only 1% of the company's small business customers churned each month.

We could infer that the company found product/market fit in the small business customer segment, but not yet in the mid-sized customer segment. Given that the company successfully pursued a low-touch acquisition approach with regard to acquiring small businesses, the unit economics worked in this specific target customer group. The founders eventually decided to accelerate growth with regard to the small business customer segment and to concentrate on generating product/market fit in the mid-sized customer segment. Only if they achieved product/market fit in this customer segment, also, they wanted to fuel the growth engine again also in this segment. Smart decision that eventually paid off.

Beware of averages, and work to understand your unit economics on a very granular level.

Refraining from Artificially Inflating Unit Economics

Understanding your unit economics on a granular level shows investors that you know what you are doing and why you do what

30   Lifetime = 1 / churn rate.

you do. You are steering your business in the direction of growth readiness, long-term profitability, and want to demonstrate a viable business model.

Most founders know the importance of strong unit economics and that these attract investors. Against this background, some founders artificially inflate their unit economics. A very short-sighted strategy.

For instance, I sometimes meet founders who do not include all marketing and sales costs into their customer acquisition costs calculation. Most often, they try to exclude brand marketing costs and argue that brand marketing costs are not incurred in order to acquire customers. This is certainly not correct. All marketing activities serve the ultimate goal of acquiring customers and improving the business economics. Otherwise, they should not be incurred in the first place. It is rather a question of time when brand marketing leads to a strong brand that attracts new customers and reduces customer acquisition costs. You can reflect this time element in your customer acquisition costs calculation by acknowledging that brand marketing costs may not directly correlate with customers acquired in the same period the brand marketing costs have been incurred. But you must not disregard these costs when calculating your customer acquisition costs. Brand marketing helps establish a strong brand that attracts new customers. You incur brand marketing costs to acquire customers.

As to the customer lifetime value, I see founders disregarding the contribution margin. For instance, some founders of software-as-a-service (SaaS) businesses calculate the customer lifetime value by multiplying the monthly recurring revenue (MRR) with their customers' average lifetime in months. Disregarding the contribution margin usually leads to a very unrealistic result. Take the Ubers, e-scooter, and food delivery companies of this world as examples. Their unit economics problems have many reasons, but they especially stem from the fact that the direct costs associated with a ride or delivery are extremely high compared to the revenue these companies generate per transaction. If you disregard the direct costs and the contribution margin, you may see strong unit economics. But they are artificially inflated. You need to consider the contribution margin when calculating your customer lifetime value.

And your contribution margin must consider *all* variable costs. Variable costs are the costs that are directly related to sales. They vary with the number of units sold. You incur such costs so that your customers can use your products and services as expected. Disregarding all costs of goods sold (CoGS) is certainly an obvious mistake some founders make. But there are other costs that some founders believe do not have to be considered. The costs incurred for shipping and packaging for an e-commerce business, the technology infrastructure costs of a platform business,[31] the delivery costs for a delivery service company, as well as customer success[32] and support costs incurred by a software-as-a-service (SaaS) company need to be considered in this regard, at least as a general rule.

31 Not the development costs in this regard.

32 To the extent not incurred in order to up- and cross sell, as such costs could be considered customer acquisition costs.

Founders who artificially inflate their unit economics either fool themselves or convey to investors they do not know how to steer their businesses. If you want to raise growth capital you should therefore calculate and report your unit economics correctly.

Being Patient

If you scale your business on strong unit economics, you accelerate growth after the fundamental elements of your business model have been validated. In contrast, if you fuel your growth engine before your unit economics are strong, you may burn through substantial cash without ever being able to demonstrate a viable business model.

Scaling your business without having been able to demonstrate strong unit economics is therefore a risky approach to growth.

Have the patience to develop strong unit economics. It is one of the hardest things to do if you want to create a high growth business. But it will eventually pay off.

. . . . .

On the basis of strong unit economics, you can grow fast and efficiently. You accelerate growth after having validated the fundamental elements of your business model, at least if your technology supports high growth. We will look into the importance of a stable, secure, and scalable technology in the next chapter.

Key Founder Takeaways

☐ The unit economics concept is a powerful tool that helps you better understand whether you pursue a viable business model. Strong unit economics tell you that the fundamental elements of your business model have been validated.

☐ Strong unit economics and short payback periods usually translate into higher profitable growth and great cash efficiency. You need to raise less cash from investors and can retain a larger stake in your company.

☐ The most common unit economics analysis looks at a single customer. You calculate the customer lifetime value and the customer acquisition costs as well as the ratio between the customer lifetime value and the customer acquisition costs.

☐ The customer lifetime value reflects the value that you extract from a customer over the customer's lifetime. In order to calculate the customer lifetime value, you have to add up all contributions stemming from a customer over the customer's lifetime.

☐ The customer acquisition costs are the total costs you incur in order to acquire a customer. You add up all marketing and sales costs you incur in a specific period of time and divide the sum by the number of new customers acquired.

☐ Calculating your payback period in terms of the time it takes until you recoup your customer acquisition costs provides additional valuable insights. The shorter your payback period, the earlier you can reinvest your customer acquisition costs into acquiring even more customers and the less money you need to grow your business.

☐ In order to calculate the payback period in months, you divide your customer acquisition costs by your customers' monthly contributions.

☐ You can improve your business and steer it towards high growth readiness by deconstructing the unit economics metrics into their components and improving each and every component.

☐ Irrespective of the business model you pursue, you need to beware of working with averages. Working with averages can be meaningless and guide you in the wrong direction.

☐ Understanding your unit economics on a granular level shows investors that you want to steer your business in the direction of growth readiness and long-term profitability.

☐ Do not artificially inflate your unit economics. Founders who artificially inflate their unit economics either fool themselves or convey to investors that they do not know how to steer their businesses.

☐ Have the patience to develop strong unit economics. It is one of the hardest things to do if you want to create a high growth business. But it will eventually pay off.

Establishing a Scalable Technology

Shipping first time code is like going into debt. A little debt speeds development so long as it is paid back promptly with a rewrite... The danger occurs when the debt is not repaid. Every minute spent on not-quite-right code counts as interest on that debt. Entire engineering organizations can be brought to a stand-still under the debt load of an unfactored[33] implementation, object-oriented or otherwise.[34]

WARD CUNNINGHAM, CO-AUTHOR OF THE 'MANIFESTO FOR AGILE DEVELOPMENT'

One day you celebrate having generated product/market fit and product/channel fit and plan for heavily fueling your growth engine. The next day you experience tech performance problems. Your customers cannot use your products and services. Or it takes your customers ages to access your services that should be available in milli-seconds. Suddenly, you

---

33   Ward Cunningham originally used the term 'unconsolidated'.

34   The WyCash Portfolio Management System / by Ward Cunningham. Retrieved from: http://c2.com/doc/oopsla92.html.

see your customers running out your doors complaining about the instability of your technology. They churn and leave bad reviews. A vicious circle leads to a shrinking business and ultimately complete failure. A horror scenario for every founder.

Despite the great importance of a scalable technology for the success of their ventures and the ability to raise growth capital, I have seen founders who fell prey to short-term thinking and continuously prioritizing the development and deployment of ever new products and product features over a balanced approach to growth.

Make sure you do not fall prey to short-term thinking. If you do not ensure that your technology infrastructure can cope with an ever-increasing load in terms of website traffic and product usage you can immediately abandon your high growth plans.

*FastScaling - **On the basis of** a relentless and company-wide focus on customer success, product/market-fit, product/channel-fit, strong unit economics, and a **scalable technology infrastructure**, efficiently and predictably leading and scaling a business fast towards market leadership in a large market.*

In a balanced approach to growth, product and tech grow in sync.

Tech Infrastructure Recap

There is no one-fits-all technology infrastructure that ensures scalability and meets the requirements of all startups. The tech infrastructure required at a fintech startup may be different from the tech infrastructure at a food delivery startup. A B2B software-as-a-service (SaaS) company may need a technology different from the technology a platform business needs. But even if companies are active in different industries, target different customer groups and segments, or pursue different business models, you can see some commonalities.

Today, most digital products are mobile or web applications. Their technical architecture can be broken down into two major parts, the frontend and the backend. The frontend is the part of the tech infrastructure that is exposed to your customers and users and hence the user interface (UI). Correspondingly, the frontend shows your customers and users the information they are supposed to see. The frontend could be a mobile app on your customers' smartphone or a website where you offer your services.

While the frontend is supposed to draw the expected content on your customers' and users' interfaces, the information shown is derived from the backend. Backend systems are providing the shared business processes and data storage. They contain databases where the information is stored and application software that works with such information and delivers it to the frontend. The frontend performance and the quality of the user experience (UX) therefore depends on the frontend software and significantly on the performance of the backend. This is why even the best user interfaces fail to deliver the expected great user experience (UX) if the backend performance is poor. If the backend performance is poor, the frontend will not manage to process the information, either fast enough or at all.

While the frontend can certainly also be a reason for a dissatisfied user experience, very often the backend performance is to be blamed, especially when the performance deteriorates after the founders have accelerated growth. Often, the backend cannot cope with the pace at which new users not only use the services, but also increase their usage. The more users and customers interact or use the services the poorer the backend performance often gets. Inevitably, this will lead to a correspondingly bad performance of the frontend and, accordingly, to a bad user experience.

You can reduce the risk of bad frontend and backend performance.

Transitioning to Microservices

One common mistake I see founders make is transitioning late from a monolithic architecture to a microservices oriented architecture.

In a monolithic architecture, all business processes, interfaces, and databases exist together in one code repository and are running together in one server environment. There is no separation among software pieces with different responsibilities and often the whole application shares one big database. Imagine a website on which customers can sign up, book, and pay for certain services. The whole application – the sign-up feature, the booking feature, and the payment feature – is built on a single code and runs in one environment that is connected to both the frontend and the database.

A monolithic architecture comes with the advantage that you can easily develop your first application with basic features. You do not need to think about interfaces among different parts of your application, since all code sits in the same environment. This way you can develop your minimal viable product (MVP), set up your server and database and launch. A very cost-effective approach. And it often works nicely in the early days of a company, which is why many founders start out on a monolithic architecture.

But the monolithic architecture comes with major disadvantages for companies that want to achieve high growth in terms of customers, users, usage, and that may have to develop and deploy various complex feature sets.

The fact that all services are tightly coupled sets boundaries to scaling a business. As all services are interconnected and interdependent, all services must function in order for the whole application to function. Correspondingly, if any of the services needs to be maintained or updated, the whole code is affected. Any change in one software component affects other parts of the code. If one component goes down, the whole application goes down and users cannot access the entire service anymore.

To continue our example, if you have to change the sign-up application, such change also affects the booking and payment applications. Again, it is all one code. If your sign-up service goes down, the whole application goes down. In such case, you have to act fast and identify and solve the problem. But identifying the problem may be difficult as you may have to review the entire code base. And until you have identified and solved the problem, your customers cannot use your services at all.

Disregarding all other disadvantages that come with having a monolithic architecture at scale, like the bottlenecks that derive from having only one connection, and single point of failure to the frontend and the database, the monolithic architecture is a suboptimal structure for most companies with complex solutions that want to scale fast.

In contrast to the monolithic architecture where all services are tightly coupled and reside in one repository that is connected to the frontend and the database, the services in a microservices environment are loosely coupled. The services can be coded, maintained, and updated independently from each other and are connected to each other via application programming interfaces (APIs) and event-based systems. The services provide individual endpoints for the frontends. And they all have their own local database to store data.

If one service is updated, this update does not affect the other services. If one service is down, the customers can still use the other services. This ensures not only fast and independent development and deployment, but also bug isolation and granular scaling. You can improve the performance of and scale only those services that you want to scale and need to improve so your technology infrastructure can cope with the increased workload that comes with heavily scaling the business. Much smarter!

In our example, the sign-up function, the booking function, and the payment function would be coded independently from each other. If new customers could not sign up for some reason, your existing customers could still use your services while your tech team could identify and solve the sign-up problem reviewing this specific code.

I recommend you thoroughly analyze which technology architecture is better suited for your business. Not only now, but also when website traffic and usage hopefully start going through the roof and revenues soar. If the microservices architecture is the right architecture for you and if you are currently working on a monolithic architecture, do not transition late.

Transitioning from a monolithic architecture to a microservices architecture is not an easy task and takes more time than you may think. You not only have to decouple tightly coupled services and rewrite code. You also have to make sure that your services do not go down and that your customers can access your services. The transition goes also hand in hand with a cultural change as to how your teams work together and what talents you need. So, do not wait.

Either begin the whole company on a microservices architecture or start transitioning now.

Writing Scalable Code

Another issue sometimes encountered during a tech due diligence is that the tech team has not put enough energy and effort into writing and maintaining scalable code.

A code is scalable if you can easily change the code or add code if your business requires this, for instance, in order to improve a service quality or to add a new feature. The lesser lines of code your teams need to touch, write, or change, if new requests arrive, the more scalable your code is. Keep it like Mark Twain who allegedly said, "If I had had more time, I would have written a shorter letter."

Experienced Chief Technology Officers (CTO) and developer teams plan for scalability and avoid the duplication of code, reduce the overall size of the code, and the number of lines of code so that the code complexity is limited. In contrast, inexperienced teams often end up with so-called spaghetti code where the code structure lacks clarity so that sometimes even the original developers have a hard time working on the code. If you identify spaghetti code, it may already be late, and you may have to pause any scaling ambitions for a long time. A clean code is a prerequisite for entering a sustainable high growth phase.

Since every piece of code is written once, but read many times, spending ten more minutes on finding meaningful names and making your code readable will save hours if not days later on. Software engineering practices like peer reviews and pair programming make sure that the development team invests enough in documentation, skill-transfer, and code scalability.

Always ensure your team keeps the code clean and makes code scalability a priority.

Moving to the Cloud

Even today, many teams still start out working on a single physical server environment, whereas there are several good reasons to start working in the cloud from day 1.

If you have found product/market fit and product/channel fit and want to scale your business, cloud hosting enables you to scale your server resources accordingly. All you need to do is buy additional server capacity and you are ready to go. On top of this additional capacity, you also buy additional security and stability. If you run your services on a single physical server and that server goes down, your services are unavailable for your customers until you have fixed the server problem. In the cloud environment, your business runs on redundant servers that enable your host to get you up and running again within seconds.

Cloud hosting facilitates stable performance reflected in high server uptime and service availability. Since you can easily adjust your server capacity, this stability is also ensured in times of increased traffic and usage.

Some founders are concerned that moving to the cloud leads to a higher data security risk. While ensuring that your technology is secure is certainly of paramount importance, moving to the cloud and working with the best cloud service providers rarely increases the security risk. Cloud hosting isolates your servers and data from any typical physical server risks like hacking, data loss, or system overloads that can, for instance, be the consequence of distributed denial of service attacks (DDoS attacks).[35] In the cloud, when a server is compromised, your host can simply switch to another server. But cyber security should definitely be on your radar. No doubt about this.

---

35   An attempt to disrupt a server by overwhelming it with a flood of traffic.

Cloud hosting is a good way to improve your tech stability, scalability, and security. If you have not started in the cloud from day 1, consider moving to the cloud before you accelerate growth.

Needless to say, migrating to the cloud requires you to plan and execute your transition strategy thoroughly. Very often, it is wise to migrate step by step.

Documenting

Another topic that regularly pops up in connection with a tech due diligence is a lack of documentation.

Sustainable high growth requires continuous development, testing, and deployment of new services as well as constant monitoring, maintaining, and updating of services. Each growth phase may have different prerequisites for growth, not only in terms of what you need to do, but also the knowledge and experience required by your team. It is therefore the rule rather than the exception that people in your development team are exchanged fast or at least that new team members need to be added at a rapid pace. They need to be able to move at your speed, not at their own.

In order to cope with this growth from a technical and personnel perspective, you must avoid a situation in which the technical knowledge, especially around code, tech infrastructure, and server configuration, sits in the hands of a few employees only. If these few employees leave, important knowledge will be gone or it may take days or weeks to find the information.

With proper documentation you can avoid this. You enable your team to find critical information quickly. When it comes to documentation, your team should go into the details and thoroughly explain not only the specific code, architecture, and server configuration situation but also the reasoning behind your tech strategy and execution.

If your team pursues a zero-tolerance, high quality documentation approach, new team members will easily be able to work on your infrastructure and code and add features, maintain and update services. This will again facilitate scaling your technology and your business.

Do not accept any compromise with regard to documentation and be alert if you hear that new hires have a hard time getting up to speed. This may be a sign that your team is not properly documenting.

Continuously Repaying Technical Debt

Development teams adopt agile software development frameworks, like Scrum and Software Kanban, so they can more quickly and predictably deliver tangible results. Pursuing the agile software development methodology requires your teams develop features end-to-end in every iteration. This way, product increments are delivered often and feedback is received early in the process. As a result, in an agile software development approach you evolve your code from iteration to iteration rather than having a big design master-plan upfront, which you execute in a waterfall development process. Each iteration, your teams revisit some code, add to it, and extend its functionality. The teams need to keep the code quality high during this process, by continuously refactoring and unifying the codebase in every iteration.

Imagine you want to launch a new product feature. In a traditional waterfall development environment, your team develops the product feature in separate phases that build on each other and lead to a big release where the customer is confronted with the new feature. Under such a waterfall development process, your teams may spend a lot of time and put tremendous effort into developing a 100% perfect product feature only to realize that the customer expectations are not met. This will not only disappoint your customers but also your development teams as they have built something that is not of value, neither for your customers, nor for your business.

In agile software development, you do not wait until you can release a perfect product. You cannot afford to wait until the product is perfect. You write the code needed to build the most important features and ship an incomplete product in order to gather customer feedback fast.

The time and money you save by taking this fast route to market can result in so-called technical debt in the sense that software does not comply with high quality technology architectural or coding requirements. Debt is the 'money and time' that you have saved by taking a short cut. But pursuing this agile approach to software development is not meant to result in bad code. You are only saving time and effort to ensure you build what your customers want. You deploy fast in order to include the customer feedback in new releases and you constantly deploy. But you need to fix what you have not yet developed perfectly.

In reality, many tech teams are overwhelmed by new product and product feature requests and founders pushing towards further developing what is needed from a business perspective. Rather than first fixing what needs to be fixed, the teams try to meet the product development requests. But if they cannot fix what needs to be fixed, they incur more and more technical debt.

Just like traditional debt, if you incur technical debt and do not pay it off, it gets tougher and tougher to repay the principal amount and the interest accrued thereon. Ensure product and tech get the same attention, and that your tech teams constantly repay technical debt. Otherwise, you risk your technology going down.

Making Scalability a Priority

The topics discussed in this chapter cannot be considered exhaustive and one can probably list many more topics and mistakes development teams make that do not focus on scalability from the very beginning. But the topics mentioned here should provide a good basis for analyzing whether your technology will support your growth plans and what you should focus on.

While software development and especially the agile software development approach is full of compromises, you cannot allow your technology to become a bottleneck. If you have not already done so, you need to make scalability a priority. Your technology needs to be scalable, stable, and secure. Scalability is not a 'nice to have', but an inevitable high growth building block.

Some founders fail to convey a strong tone from the top as to making scalability a priority from the start. Don't be among those founders. Set the scene and bring in the right people and hold them accountable as to high standards, quality, and speed.

If you started out dreaming of establishing a high growth business, achieving a massive valuation, and retaining a significant shareholding in your company, the time to think about and plan for scale was when your team wrote your first line of code. If you have not planned for scalability at that time, the time is now.

• • • • •

If you have generated product/market fit, created product/ channel fit, and established a secure, stable, and scalable technology, you should also experience strong unit economics. You are almost ready to FastScale and fuel the growth engine. But be sure your target market is as large as you think it is. Often, founders are overly optimistic in this regard. We will discuss how to accurately size your market and why to strive for market leadership in the next chapter.

Key Founder Takeaways

☐ You should succeed or fail based on the viability of your business model and your ability to solve a significant customer problem. You must not eventually fail because you have neglected sustainable high growth requires a stable, secure, and scalable technology.

☐ Many founders fall prey to short-term thinking and prioritizing the development and deployment of ever new products and product features over a balanced approach to growth where product and tech grow in sync.

☐ Thoroughly analyze which technology architecture is best suited for your business. Not only now, but also when website traffic and usage go through the roof and revenues soar.

☐ As a general rule, the monolithic architecture is a suboptimal structure for most companies with complex solutions that want to scale fast. If you want to build a high growth business, the microservices architecture is likely the right architecture for you. If you currently work on a monolithic architecture, do not transition late.

☐ Ensure your tech teams write clean code. Avoid the

duplication of code, reduce the overall size of the code and the number of lines of code so that code complexity is limited. A clean code is a prerequisite for entering a sustainable high growth phase.

☐ Since every piece of code is written once, but read many times, spending ten more minutes on finding meaningful names and making your code readable will save hours if not days later on. Software engineering practices like peer reviews and pair programming make sure that the development team invests enough in documentation, skill-transfer, and code scalability.

☐ Cloud hosting is a good way to improve your tech stability, security, and scalability. If you have not started in the cloud from day 1, consider moving to the cloud before you accelerate growth.

☐ In order to cope with high growth from a technical and personnel perspective, you must avoid a situation in which the technical knowledge, especially around code, tech infrastructure and server configuration, sits in the hands of a few employees only. If these few employees leave, important knowledge will be gone or it will take days or weeks to find the information. Thorough documentation is key.

☐ Many tech teams are overwhelmed by new product

and product feature requests and founders pushing towards further developing what is needed from a business perspective. Ensure product and tech get the same attention and that your tech teams can constantly repay technical debt. Otherwise, you risk your technology going down.

☐ If you started out dreaming of establishing a high growth business, achieving a massive valuation and retaining a significant shareholding in your company, the time to think about and plan for scale was when your team wrote your fist line of code. If you have not planned for scalability at that time, the time is now.

☐ Make tech scalability a priority!

CHAPTER 8

Striving for Market Leadership in a Large Market

We have always focused on the market — the size of the market, the dynamics of the market, the nature of the competition — because our objective always was to build big companies. If you don't attack a big market, it's highly unlikely you're ever going to build a big company.[36]

DON VALENTINE, FOUNDER OF SEQUOIA CAPITAL

"The market is not as large as you think it is."

Rarely well-received, this message often conveys the truth.

You probably think you know how to do a proper market sizing and how large your market is. But don't be over-confident in this regard.

---

36   Target Big Markets / by Don Valentine. Retrieved from: https://www.youtube.com/watch?v=nKN-abRJMEw.

I am currently involved in a high growth business that considers accelerating growth by selling into an additional market, the care home segment of the health care market. The founders retrieved publicly available data that showed an attractive health care market. In the board of directors meeting, they wanted to get the green light to hiring for and selling into this new market. On the basis of the data provided, however, the board could not give green light. The data provided was not concerning the key target customer segment of mid-sized companies but included also small businesses and potential enterprise customers. Further, the data concerned the complete health care market and did not focus on the sub-segment of care homes. The board asked the founders to be more diligent and to come up with a proper market sizing, bottom-up, and showing the total addressable market (TAM), the serviceable addressable market (SAM), and the serviceable obtainable market (SOM), with regard to the key target customer group of mid-sized care home businesses. When the founders completed the respective analysis, they realized the number of potential key target customers was not as impressive as they had assumed it to be on the basis of the publicly available data.

*FastScaling - On the basis of a relentless and company-wide focus on customer success, product/market-fit, product/channel-fit, strong unit economics, and a scalable technology infrastructure, efficiently and predictably leading and scaling a business fast towards **market leadership in a large market**.*

But the market seemed reasonably attractive. Board and founders therefore agreed on pursuing this expansion strategy, but with a growth approach less aggressive than originally suggested by the management team, and highly focused.

It is too early to tell whether this move will pay off, but this example shows that you cannot be too diligent when it comes to sizing the market. Market sizing needs to be done prudently before you start a venture and whenever you want to enter new territories in terms of geographies, markets and customer segments, or new products and product features. If your target market is not large enough, you are bound to fail. You may be able to acquire some first customers and early adopters, but your stream of leads to your key target customers will ebb away fast.

Understanding the size of your market is therefore of utmost importance. Let us look at how to properly size a market.

Starting with Your Target Customers

Any market analysis needs to start with your key target customers. We have already discussed why a focus on your key target customers is so important if you want to create a high growth business efficiently and how to define your key target customers. You may have another look into Chapter 4 in this regard.

Measuring the Total Addressable Market (TAM)

If you have defined your key target customers, you can start calculating your total addressable market (TAM). In essence, the total addressable market equals the annual revenues[37] that your business could make if it achieved a 100% market share in your key target market.

There are essentially two approaches to calculating your total addressable market: the top-down approach and the bottom-up approach.

The Top-Down Approach

Under the top-down market sizing approach, you analyze the size of the market on the basis of publicly available data such as industry reports. An industry report could, for instance, reveal that the size of a specific European market is €7bn. If you can find trustworthy, reputable, and authoritative data on how big your key target market is, this can be a very valid starting point for your market sizing efforts. But you must make sure that the publicly available data indeed focuses on your key target market and key market segments.

For example, as I have been investing in B2B companies active in consumer industries, I have often looked at companies selling software solutions to restaurants. While there is certainly a great number of restaurants out there, the market can get pretty small pretty fast if you accurately define your key target customers.

Firstly, you need to come up with valid data concerning the specific key target customer segment of the restaurant industry that you want to serve. If you sell only to small independent restaura-

37   Or gross profit.

teurs, you cannot work with publicly available data as to the number of independent entrepreneurs, as independent restaurateurs are only a subsegment of this bigger target customer group of independent entrepreneurs. You cannot work with numbers regarding the restaurant industry in general, either, as these numbers also concern mid-sized restaurants and restaurant chains. Publicly available data like 'the foodservice market in Europe is worth $500 billion' is also a dangerous starting point. Firstly, this dollar amount tells you what restaurants and food services make in terms of revenue, but not how much they spend on software. Secondly, this data refers to restaurants and food services and does not concern your key target customers of independent restaurateurs only.

You would start from a more trustworthy basis if you additionally found reputable data on how much of their revenues restaurateurs spend on their tech and, even better, on the specific software solutions you sell. Maybe you can also directly access information that restaurateurs spend some €2 billion on software solutions similar to yours.

From this data point, you still have to work with certain assumptions regarding how much is spent by your key target customer group. If you additionally found data telling you that 50% of all food service outlets were small independent restaurants, you might infer that your total addressable market amounts to some €1 billion (€2 billion * 50%).

With accurate and trustworthy information concerning your target market and key target customers, the top-down approach can provide you with a good first data point as to the size of your total addressable market. But I recommend you definitely pursue the bottom-up approach. The bottom-up approach to market sizing is the approach most investors prefer.

The Bottom-Up Approach

The bottom-up approach forces you to critically think about how many key target customers are in your target market and how much they will spend on your products and services. Multiplying the number of key target customers in your target market with the annual revenues such customers generate on average will yield the total addressable market under the bottom-up approach.

Your starting point is the number of key target customers in your target market. In order to get to this number, you can again look for publicly available data telling you how many key target customers exist. For instance, you may find data telling you that there are two million food service outlets in Europe. Basing your market sizing on this number may again be difficult and inaccurate as your key target customers have very specific characteristics that are not fully reflected in such publicly available data. But if you could reasonably assume that 50% of such outlets were independent restaurants, you would end up with one million European key target customers.

Given the often inaccuracy of publicly available data, you should additionally analyze and prioritize your internal data. In our above example, you may have data available about how many key target customers you have found in a specific city, region, or country. And you may be able to extrapolate this number in order to estimate the number of key target customers in Europe. If you know that there are 200,000 food service outlets in Germany, but only 40,000 match your key target customer criteria, you may conclude that the relevant ratio of key target customers to food outlets is rather closer to 20% (40,000/200,000), which would lead to a total number of European key target customers of 400,000 (2 million * 20%).[38]

In order to get to the total addressable market, you now need to multiply the number of key target customers with your average revenue per key target customer per year.

Assuming that you charge each customer €100 in monthly recurring revenues (MRR), and hence €1,200 per year, you will end up with a total addressable market of €480 million (€1,200 * 400,000). Now, this is far away from the size of the market that your top-down approach has generated.

Triangulating Your Research Results

Using the top-down approach and the bottom-up approach to market sizing, you generated at least two results in terms of how large your total addressable market could be. If you can reasonably trust your data points, you may triangulate your research results using your intuition. Do not be overly optimistic. If you underestimate your market, you may be positively surprised by the actual size of your target market. Better be conservative than surprised negatively later on.

---

38   Certainly, assuming that the ratio is similar in other European countries, which you should validate.

In our example, if you believe the truth lies somewhere in the middle and you have some confidence in the number stemming from your top-down approach, you may triangulate and include the top-down numbers in your overall assessment. In such case, you could assume that your total addressable market is $740m ((€1bn + €480 million)/2).

But be sure you can indeed triangulate and work with averages. Your investors will ask how you got to that number and will check the underlying assumptions. You should have good answers. Furthermore, you must not forget you do the market sizing not to impress venture capital investors but, and even more so, in order to steer your business in the right direction. If you artificially inflate your market size or just be overly optimistic, you fool yourself.

I will never forget an Austrian founder saying: "Well, you know what, Patrick, the number on our pitch deck is only supposed to be an eye catcher. We have not really analyzed the size of the market. We know it is large."

If in doubt, you should trust your bottom-up numbers. In our example, this would lead to a total addressable market of €480 million.

Measuring the Serviceable Addressable Market (SAM)

It is, however, important to think not only about the total addressable market, but also about how much of this total addressable market you can actually serve given your industry, market, company, and business model specifics.

While the actual steps that must be taken in order to get from your total addressable market to your serviceable addressable market (SAM) highly depend on your company and industry specifics, let me point towards a few topics you should at least consider.

Have a thorough look at your go-to-market strategy and consider the channels to your customers that work and where you have found product/channel fit. Reduce the number of potential target customers by the number of customers you cannot reach given your go-to-market strategy. For instance, if you pursue an inbound marketing and an inside sales approach leading to a low-touch customer acquisition strategy, you may reduce the number of customers you can serve by the number of customers who expect a high touch acquisition and onboarding approach.

Consider your business model specifics. For instance, you may pursue a platform business model characterized by a need to scale both the demand and the supply side. If you can find demand almost everywhere but supply only in some areas (e.g. major cities), reduce your serviceable market accordingly.

Whatever your business model, industry, market, and customer characteristics, make sure you do not overestimate how many of your theoretically addressable key target customers you can, in fact, service before you go to the next step and calculate your serviceable obtainable market (SOM).

Measuring the Serviceable Obtainable Market (SOM)

It goes without saying that investors look for companies that become market leaders, and you should certainly strive for market leadership. But even market leaders do not capture 100% of their serviceable addressable market (SAM). Some potentially serviceable addressable customers will decide to buy competitive products or refrain from buying at all. Your serviceable obtainable market (SOM) will be a fraction of your serviceable addressable market.

While many founders work with estimates and, for instance, assume they can capture 30% of the serviceable addressable market, you should also apply some methodology here.

You may, for example, look at your conversion rate that nicely shows how many leads to your key target customers you need to generate in order to acquire a customer. If your conversion rate is 30% and if you can validate that you will be able to reach all serviceable customers over time, you may indeed work with the assumption that you can obtain 30% of your serviceable addressable market.

One of the major concerns many investors have is that a company is unable to generate any barriers to entry fending off potential competitors. Never underestimate your competitors. Keep your friends close and your enemies closer. Follow them closely and understand their strategy and what makes you unique and keeps you unique. Take competition into account when sizing your serviceable obtainable market.

As a last step, you should also double-check whether your business plan goals in terms of revenues you want to generate over time are backed up by your market analysis. You need to validate that your serviceable obtainable market is not smaller than the revenues you want to generate according to your business plan.

Considering Specific Market Characteristics & Dynamics

The market attractiveness does not only depend on its sheer size, but also on the margins you can generate and the market dynamics. You should include these aspects into your market sizing efforts.

Certainly, investors like startups targeting a market in which they can create high margin businesses. A good example is the software-as-a-service (SaaS) industry in which you can see gross margins of some 80% and EBITDA margins of some 40%.

As to market dynamics, you really need to analyze how your market is going to evolve. If you raise growth capital, you have already proven that there is a market for your products. But how is this market going to evolve. Have your revenues already peaked? Is the market saturated? Is the market size decreasing? Or are you targeting a large and growing market that will be even larger when you exit?

Most investors are obsessed with the size of your target market. You should be, too.

Striving for Market Leadership

Over time, most tech markets become 'winner-takes-it-all markets', in which you see one dominant market leader and some insignificant followers. Even if your target market may be different and allow for more than one big company, your assumption should always be that it may end up being a 'winner-takes-it-all market', in which you want to be the market leader. If you capture most of your target market, you will not have difficulties generating cash and raising additional cash from investors. With such resources, you should be able to defend and further expand your market share, create competitive moats, and develop new innovative products that you can sell to your existing customer base and new customers that you can acquire based on a strong brand.

Acquirers pay significant premiums for market leaders. If you can create this kind of market leader in a large market, you are on track to building a massively valuable business. Winning your market is key.

Strive for market leadership!

• • • • •

We have meanwhile looked at all five building blocks representing a solid FastScaling foundation. Let's ignite growth and FastScale. FastScaling is not about simply adding marketing and sales resources. You do not create sustainable high growth by focusing only on top line growth. If you FastScale, customer success needs to be your north star. Let us therefore turn to the next chapter and see how you make your customers incredibly successful and what impact this will have on your growth trajectory.

Key Founder Takeaways

☐ "The market is not as large as you think it is." Rarely well-received, this message often conveys the truth.

☐ If your target market is not large enough, you may be able to acquire some first customers and early adopters, but your stream of leads to your key target customers will ebb away fast.

☐ If you have clearly defined your key target customers, you can start calculating your total addressable market (TAM). In essence, the total addressable market equals the annual revenues that your business could make if it achieved a 100% market share in your key target market.

☐ There are essentially two approaches to calculating your total addressable market: the top-down approach and the bottom-up approach.

☐ Under the top-down approach to market sizing, you analyze the size of the market on the basis of publicly available data such as industry reports. If you can find trustworthy, reputable, and authoritative data on how big your key target market is, this can be a very valid starting point for your market sizing efforts.

☐ The bottom-up approach forces you to critically think about how many key target customers are in your target market and how much they will spend on your products and services per year. Multiplying the number of key target customers in your target market with the annual revenues such customers generate on average will yield the total addressable market under the bottom-up approach.

☐ Using the top-down approach and the bottom-up approach to market sizing, you generated at least two results in terms of how large your total addressable market could be. If you can reasonably trust your data points, you may triangulate your research results using your intuition. Do not be overly optimistic. If you underestimate your market, you may be positively surprised by the actual bigger number of key target customers in your target market. Better be conservative than surprised negatively later on. If in doubt, trust your bottom-up approach numbers.

☐ It is important to think not only about the total addressable market, but also about how much of this total addressable market you can actually serve given your industry, market, company, and business model specifics as well as the time until you want to exit.

☐ While the actual steps you need to take in order to get from your total addressable market to your serviceable addressable market (SAM) highly depend on your company and industry specifics, you should at least consider your go-to-market approach and other business model specifics. You must exclude all customers you cannot access given these peculiarities.

☐ Even market leaders do not capture 100% of their serviceable addressable market. Your serviceable obtainable market (SOM) will be a fraction of your serviceable addressable market. Do not work with any rule of thumb but apply some sophistication and methodology. You may, for instance, consider your conversion rate.

☐ The market attractiveness not only depends on its sheer size, but also on the margins that you can generate and the market dynamics.

☐ As to market dynamics, you need to analyze how your market is going to evolve. Have revenues already peaked? Is the market saturated? Is the market size decreasing? Or are you targeting a large and growing market that will be even larger when you exit?

☐ Most investors are obsessed with the size of your target market. You should be, too.

☐ Strive for market leadership! Market leaders can achieve high valuation premiums. If you can create a market leader in a large market, you are on track to building a massively valuable business.

FastScaling

CHAPTER 9

Focusing on Customer Success

Your customers don't care about you. They don't care about your product or service. They care about themselves, their dreams, their goals. Now, they will care much more if you help them reach their goals, and to do that, you must understand their goals, as well as their needs and deepest desires.

STEVE JOBS, FOUNDER OF APPLE

You have established the FastScaling foundation and validated the fundamental elements of your business model. You have found product/market fit and a channel through which you can sell your products on attractive economic terms. Your technology is stable, secure, and scalable, and you are looking at a large market ready to be conquered. Your unit economics confirm you are ready to FastScale.

FastScaling is more than accelerating growth by adding marketing and sales resources.

You do not create a sustainable high growth business and achieve a massive valuation by simply adding more and more marketing and sales resources. Your customer needs and preferences constantly change and evolve. Product/market fit and product/channel fit are short-lived if you do not constantly adapt and focus on making your customers successful.

Scale your business with a relentless and company-wide focus on customer success and revenue growth will follow magically.

Customer Success & Unit Economics

Customer success significantly impacts your unit economics.

If your customers experience a strong return on investment and have a great customer experience, your customers' willingness to pay will reflect this in a positive way. Your customers' higher willingness to pay will positively impact your average revenue per customer and correspondingly your customer lifetime value.

If your customers are highly satisfied, they will also be primed for up- and cross-sells, which will further increase the average revenue per customer and your customer lifetime value.

If you solve your customer problems in a differentiated way and better than your competition, your customers will stick around and churn less. Your customer retention and customer lifetime expand correspondingly. Higher contribution over a longer period of time translate into an even higher customer lifetime value.

At the same time, your customer acquisition costs will improve too. If your customers get a strong return on investment and have a fantastic customer experience, they become your advocates, write great reviews, and refer your products and services to more customers. Your brand recognition and your brand value will rise, which will facilitate your marketing and sales efforts and ultimately improve your conversion funnel. You will see you can generate more high-quality leads that you can successfully convert into even more highly satisfied customers. Your customer acquisition costs go down.

As the average customer contribution increases and the customer acquisition costs decrease, you can shorten your payback period. You can reinvest faster into acquiring even more customers.

*FastScaling - **On the basis of a relentless and company-wide focus on customer success**, product/ market-fit, product/ channel-fit, strong unit economics, and a scalable technology infrastructure, efficiently and predictably leading and scaling a business fast towards market leadership in a large market.*

As we have seen in Chapter 6, strong unit economics and short payback periods translate into higher profitable growth and great cash efficiency. You need to raise less cash from investors and can retain a larger stake in your company.

Make your customers incredibly successful and you will see a strong improvement in your unit economics, growth rate, and cash efficiency.

Customer Success & Your Key Target Customers

Making your customers successful starts with focusing on

the right target audience. As we have already seen in connection with generating product/market fit, generating product/channel fit, and analyzing the size of your target market, it is of paramount importance that you accurately segment your market and clearly define your key target customers. Focus solely on your key target customers and disregard all other potential customers.

Do not spend time acquiring other potential customers or making non-key target customers happy. Trying to acquire and please these customers is useless. You will fail. Time, efforts, and money spent will not pay off. The contrary is true. Your products do not perfectly solve the problems these customers have. A lower willingness to pay will be the consequence. They will be less prone for up- and cross-sell. As they will not be truly satisfied with your products, they will also churn faster. A shorter retention rate will lead to a shorter customer lifetime and a worse customer lifetime value. It will also be more difficult to convince them to buy in the first place. A worse conversion rate will lead to a deterioration in customer acquisition costs. Lower customer contribution over a shorter period of time as well as higher customer acquisition costs. Less growth and a higher cash burn are the consequences. Make sure your teams do not spend time on potential customers other than your key target customers.

If you have clearly defined your key target customers, you need to understand their needs, preferences, and expectations. What do they expect in terms of a strong return on investment and what constitutes a great customer experience for them? Jeff Bezos put it this way: "We start with the customer and we work backwards."[39]

In my discussions with founders, I have noticed that customer success is very often perceived as a function responsible for activating, onboarding, and supporting customers. This narrow understanding of customer success won't do the trick. Customer success should be your mantra. The complete organization should work towards customer success. Only if product, engineering, marketing, sales, and customer success teams jointly strive for making your customers incredibly successful, you are on track. And only if your business intelligence and finance people accurately understand what customer success means and measure the underlying metrics, you can drive your organization towards ultimate success, not only customer success but also your business success.

Customer success is a company-wide endeavor.

Customer Success & Product

If customer success is the north star, your VP of Product or Chief Product Officer (CPO) must lead your product team towards this north star. She needs to closely work together with all other teams on gathering enough information, so the product team clearly understands what the key target customers expect in terms of return on investment and customer experience.

The missing pieces need to find their way into the product roadmap that should prioritize products and product features in

39   We Start With the Customer and We Work Backward. Jeff Bezos on Amazon's Success / by Daniel Lyons. Retrieved from: https://slate.com/news-and-politics/2009/12/jeff-bezos-on-amazon-s-success.html.

light of their impact on customer success. I usually see three overarching topics that you, as a founder, should discuss with your VP of Product or Chief Product Officer.

Firstly, you need to discuss and understand your current product offering and what needs to be developed in order to achieve or improve customer success.

Secondly, you must reach a common understanding that you deal with product cycles. Your customer needs and preferences evolve over time. You have to jointly ensure that you retain product/market fit even if your customers' preferences and needs change. A company that does not innovate is bound to fail. This is not only true for big corporations, but also for startups and scale-ups. You have to constantly reinvent yourself in order to excel in an ever faster changing market environment and to fend off competition.

Thirdly, watch out for signs that your product teams have fallen in love with your products and product features in the sense that they want to develop products and product features that are nice-to-have or only a few customers have requested. As you want to grow efficiently and avoid any unnecessary founder dilution stemming from unnecessary funding rounds, you must ensure that each dollar spent on product and product feature development has a corresponding business impact. Customization and complexity are growth killers. Understand your product roadmap!

In my experience from working with founders, it has always been helpful to ask your product teams to clarify the *why* in this regard. Ask them to write down the reasoning behind their product development requests. Why is this product or product feature significantly improving your key target customers' return on investment or customer experience? What is the business impact in measurable numbers? This request makes it easier for you to understand the reasoning behind your teams' product development plans and forces your product teams to repeatedly think about customer success and business success.

Customer Success & Technology

In light of ensuring customer success, your development team is responsible for delivering on the product roadmap and making sure that your technology is stable, secure, and scalable.

In my experience, this leads to one typical conflict you need to successfully get beyond. While the product teams ask the development teams to develop new products and product features, the Chief Technology Officer (CTO) also needs to ensure technology security, stability, and scalability and repay technical debt.

As a founder, you must intervene here. Yes, you want to delight your customers and you may feel pressure to deliver the next product or product feature. And yes, you need to be innovative. But you must avoid short-term thinking. A scalable technology is a FastScaling building block and an essential part of a solid FastScaling foundation. Establishing and retaining the FastScaling foundation should always have the highest priority. The fundamental elements need to be in place at any time. If your technology cannot cope with growth and goes bust, you go bust, too.

If you sense tension between your Chief Technology Officer (CTO) and your Chief Product Officer (CPO), dig deep into the problem and understand their arguments. If you believe that technology stability, security, or scalability may indeed be or have become an issue, bolster your Chief Technology Officer, and prioritize technology stability, security, and scalability.

Certainly, this is not always black and white and sometimes it may be the right advice to prioritize product and product feature development. But, as a founder, you must give guidance to your product and engineering teams that product development and tech stability, security, and scalability go hand in hand. Only then, you can scale your company successfully and be successful yourself in the long run.

Customer Success & Marketing and Sales

You have, meanwhile, a clear understanding of what your key target customers expect. Make sure your respective understanding is the basis for all your marketing and sales activities. Your marketing messages, the material you provide to your customers throughout the customer journey, and the dialogues your marketing and sales teams have with your customers, must authentically align with your key target customers' needs and expectations.

If you pursue a content marketing strategy, your content must relate to your customers' pain points and the return on investment your customers expect. If you want to generate website visitors, you need landing pages for each key target customer group and potential sub-group. Your website content, messages, and calls to action need to be tailored accordingly. If you are active in several countries where your customers speak different languages, you must make sure that you not only translate your English marketing content into the relevant other languages. People in different countries usually live in different cultures. Your target customers may not only have different needs but also different expectations in terms of how they want to be targeted. Start with your key target customers in each industry, segment, or geography and work backwards. Customize your marketing activities accordingly.

As soon as your marketing teams personally interact with your potential customers, the interactions have to focus on the specific customer pain point and expectation. Personalization is key. Your marketing manager must work to understand what the specific customer expects from the purchase of your product. And she needs to have the right marketing material for this customer at this customer touchpoint. The knowledge gathered must be stored and accessible for all teams that continue working with this customer. You want to avoid a situation in which customers are handed over from marketing to sales without the content of the previous discussions being accessible to your sales teams. You can be sure that your customers appreciate if they do not have to tell the same story over and over again. Your sales teams do not start from scratch again but already know the characteristics of the customer to whom they speak.

The focus on customer success does not end with the sale of your products. Customer success will also drive your activation, onboarding, and support activities. The customer journey needs to be seamless.

Customer Success & Activation, Onboarding and Support

Your marketing and sales teams work on attracting potential customers and guiding them through the conversion funnel towards the closing of a deal. Depending on the business model you pursue, a customer success team may then take over in order to activate, onboard, and support your customers. This especially holds true for B2B companies.

In connection with activating, onboarding, and supporting your customers, the customer experience component of customer success and a short time to value must be in focus, meaning the customer must see a strong return on investment quickly.

You want to activate and onboard your customers as smoothly and fast as possible. If you manage to provide a great activation and onboarding experience and deliver on your value proposition promise fast, you will notice fast product adoption and satisfied customers. When I work with founders who manage to improve the activation and onboarding experience, I usually see a corresponding improvement of the early churn rate and the customer retention rate, respectively. Better churn and retention rates positively impact the customer lifetime length and hence the customer lifetime value.

As to your support function, you must similarly combine a great customer support experience with a short time to solution. If you smoothly provide a fast solution to your customer problems, you will satisfy your customers who continue using your product and do not look for competitive products. Less churn and higher customer retention.

Your investments into your customer success team should therefore significantly impact your unit economics and revenue growth rate. At the same time, you must be conscious about the fact that the costs associated with activation, onboarding, and support are usually costs of goods sold (CoGS), which reduce your contribution margin and thus your customer lifetime value. You, therefore, need to find the right balance between the costs you incur and the business impact you see. Ultimately, your goal should be to improve your customers' activation, onboarding, and support experience as much as possible with as little as possible increase in costs. Discuss with your product, engineering, and customer success teams whether you can develop in-product solutions or buy third-party software solutions that enable you to serve your customers in a low-touch or even no-touch manner. Remember, human touch points are expensive. But, again, the ultimate goal must be customer success. Do not reduce human touch if this leads to a worse customer experience and satisfaction.

Measuring Customer Success

Given the impact that customer success has on all variables underlying your unit economics and therefore on your growth trajectory and external financing need, it is important that you measure customer success and steer your business accordingly in a data-driven manner.

If you generate a strong return on investment and a great customer experience, you should see improvements with regard to many customer and company related metrics. Customer success should lead to improved product usage and engagement as well as higher customer and revenue retention rates. You should also see an increasing number of customer referrals and good product and company reviews. Cross- and up-sells increase your average revenue per customer. Organic growth channels may lead to reduced customer acquisition costs. Measure what matters at your company in this regard. Ultimately, improved customer success should go hand in hand with improved unit economics.

In addition, you may also look at the development of your net promoter score, the customer health score (CHS), and the product stickiness metric that we discussed in Chapter 4 in connection with measuring product/market fit. The more successful you make your customers, the better your respective scores and metrics should get. And there are additional tools you may refer to in order to measure customer success.

The customer effort score (CES) measures how much effort a customer must put into the interactions with your company. The ultimate goal underlying this scale is to offer customers a more seamless experience. You ask your customers, "How much effort did it take to deal with us?" Your customers can reply marking on a scale of 1 to 5. Alternatively, you could state, "The company made it easy for me to handle my issue." Then, ask your customers to respond with the ratings varying from 'strongly disagree' to 'strongly agree'.

The customer effort score can especially help you measure your customer experience if you use it at specific touchpoints where the effort question is really relevant. In my experience, good use cases can be the onboarding, activation, and support services you provide.

The customer satisfaction score (CSAT) measures customer satisfaction by asking, "How satisfied were you with your experience?" There is a corresponding survey scale that varies from company to company. I have seen scales ranging from 1 to 3, 1 to 10 and anything in between. This type of survey allows customers to give feedback at various touch points along the customer journey and about the overall customer satisfaction.

Whatever metric or score you use in order to measure customer success, do not focus on improving metrics. Instead focus on improving customer success. If you make your customers incredibly successful, your metrics and scores will follow.

Customer Success & Exit Valuation

There is a strong correlation between a relentless and company-wide focus on customer success and the exit valuation you can achieve. A focus on customer success leads to improved unit economics as well as higher growth and less cash burn. You grow faster and more efficiently. This translates into a more attractive company for which buyers are willing to pay a higher purchase price.

The following software-as-a-service (SaaS) company example can shed more light on this correlation, the correlation between a relentless focus on customer success and exit valuation. It is supposed to showcase the impact of customer churn, expansion revenues (up- and cross-sell), and referrals on the growth and exit valuation potential of a hypothetical software-as-a-service (SaaS) company. You can find the respective Excel file at www.fastscaling.io.[40]

The Base Case

Let us assume this hypothetical company has 500 existing customers who pay $1,000 in monthly recurring revenues (MRR). Correspondingly, the company has $500,000 in monthly recurring revenues and $6,000,000 in annual recurring revenues (ARR).

Each month, this company spends $50,000 on sales and marketing and acquires 50 new customers each generating $1,000 new monthly recurring revenues. This translates into $50,000 in new business monthly recurring revenues per month and $600,000 in new business annual recurring revenues. Each month, the company

---

40   The Correlation between Customer Success and Exit Valuation / by Patrick Flesner.
      Retrieved from: https://www.fastscaling.io/customer-success-impact-on-growth-
      and-exit-valuation/.

loses 1% of its existing customer base. It does not manage to generate any expansion revenues or referrals.

In month 72, this company has 2,816 customers, $22,000 in net new business monthly recurring revenues[41], $2,816,000 in total monthly recurring revenues (MRR) and $33,792,000 in total annual recurring revenues.

Software-as-a-service companies are usually valued based on an ARR multiple. Let us assume a fair market multiple is 5. This translates into a company valuation of $168,960,000 (5 * $33,792,000).

The Bad Case

If the same company experiences a 4% monthly customer churn rate (not 1%), the growth quickly flattens out. The monthly recurring revenues churn stemming from churning customers almost completely eats up new business monthly recurring revenues.[42]

This company ends up with only $2,000 in net new business monthly recurring revenues in month 72. It has 1,210 customers, $1,210,000 in monthly recurring revenues and $14,520,000 in annual recurring revenues.

Artificially assuming that the market does not penalize less growth and also applies an annual recurring revenues multiple of 5, the company valuation is only $72,600,000 (5 * $14,520,000).

---

41   New business MRR plus expansion MRR minus MRR churn minus MRR contraction.

42   The bigger the MRR base the bigger the MRR churn and the more MRR you need to acquire to make up for MRR churn.

The Good Case

In the good case, the company still cannot prevent that some customers churn. It still experiences 1% in monthly customer churn. But is able to achieve a monthly up- and cross-sell rate of 1%. The company has 2,816 customers and achieves approximately $40,000 in net new monthly recurring revenues in month 72. This is almost $20,000 more than in the base case.

The company shows $4,097,740 in monthly recurring revenues and $49,172,884 in annual recurring revenues translating into an exit valuation of $245,864,418 (5 * $49,172,884).

The Best Case

And finally, the best case. This company resembles some characteristics of software-as-a-service (SaaS) companies that have become unicorns. 1% is the magic number. 1% monthly customer churn rate, 1% monthly up- and cross-sell rate and a 1% referral rate.[43]

This company achieves monthly net new business recurring revenues of $90,303 in month 72, total monthly recurring revenues of $5,734,194 and annual recurring revenues of $68,810,331 translating into an exit valuation of $344,051,656 (5 * $68,810,331).

Conclusion

This very simplified theoretical example demonstrates that the

---

43   Meaning that on a monthly basis new customers can be added representing 1% of the existing customer base.

long-term health of your company, your growth trajectory, and your exit valuation potential depend on how successful you make your customers. If you make them incredibly successful, customer churn will be low. You will experience strong revenue growth and retention, compelling up- and cross-sell revenues and many customer referrals. This translates into strong unit economics and high and very efficient growth. You must raise less cash and can retain a higher stake in your company. You own more of the company you have founded when you sell it on the basis of a massive company exit valuation.

This example has disregarded many more benefits associated with a relentless and company-wide focus on customer success. In particular, the annual recurring revenues multiples potential acquirers are willing to apply heavily depend on the size of the market, the growth of a business and the efficiency with which the founders scale the business. In fact, the exit valuation would differ even more as the market would apply even higher revenue multiples to the good case and best case companies.

Leading with a Strong Tone from the Top

Striving for customer success requires a strong tone from the top. Customer success needs to be more than lip service. You need to act accordingly. If you, as the leader, only care about the next four weeks revenues, do not be surprised if the whole organization only cares about the next four weeks revenues. If you cannot see any customer success relevant metric on the dashboards you place all over your office space, no wonder nobody in your organization puts the customer first.

As a founder, you need to guide your teams towards your north star. Customer success. Walk the talk!

• • • • •

With a relentless and company-wide focus on customer success, you can now fuel the growth engine and generate predictable revenues. We will discuss how to generate predictable revenues in the next chapter.

Key Founder Takeaways

☐ Your customers' needs evolve. And their preferences may change in terms of the channels through which they want to be found and acquired. Product/market fit and product/channel fit may be short-lived if you do not constantly adapt and focus on making your customers successful.

☐ You make your customers successful if they have a strong return on their investment and a great customer experience.

☐ Focus solely on making your key target customers successful. Disregard all non-key target customers. Trying to acquire and please the non-key target customers is useless. You will fail. Time, efforts, and money spent will not pay off.

☐ Making your customers successful starts with understanding the needs and expectations of your key target customers. What means a strong return on investment and a great customer experience for them?

☐ From a product perspective, you need to understand what products and product features need to be developed in order to achieve and retain customer success. Be on top of the product roadmap.

☐ But watch out for signs that your product teams have fallen in love with your products and product features in the sense that they want to develop products and product features that are 'nice-to-have' or only a few customers have requested. Ensure that each dollar spent on product and product feature development has a corresponding business impact. Customization and complexity are growth killers.

☐ As a founder, you must give guidance to your Chief Technology Officer (CTO) and your Chief Product Officer (CPO) that product development and tech stability, security, and scalability must go hand in hand.

☐ Make sure the needs and expectations of your key target customers are the basis for all your marketing and sales activities.

☐ As soon as your marketing and sales teams personally interact with your potential customers, the interactions have to focus on the specific customer pain point and expectation. Personalization is key.

☐ The focus on customer success does not end with the sale of your products. Customer success will also have to drive your activation, onboarding, and support activities. The customer journey needs to be seamless.

☐ From a customer experience point of view, you want to activate, onboard, and support your customers as smoothly and fast as possible.

☐ From a return on investment perspective, the customer success team should achieve a short time to value. The sooner you deliver on your value proposition promise the better.

☐ If you generate a strong return on investment and a great customer experience, you should see improvements with regard to many customer and company related metrics. Track them relentlessly.

☐ There is a strong correlation between a relentless and company-wide focus on customer success and the exit valuation you can achieve. If you make your customers incredibly successful, customer churn will be low. You will experience strong revenue growth and retention, compelling up- and cross-sell revenues and many customer referrals. This translates into strong unit economics and high and very efficient growth. You must raise less cash and can retain a higher stake in your company. You own more of the company you have founded when you sell it on the basis of a massive company exit valuation.

☐ You must be the role model and lead with a strong tone from the top in terms of prioritizing customer success across the organization. Walk the talk!

CHAPTER 10

Growing Predictably

Of course, you want more revenue, but what good is it if it isn't predictable?[44]

AARON ROSS, AUTHOR OF 'PREDICTABLE REVENUE'

There is an invisible hand magically connecting customer success and revenue growth. But you still need growth teams who acquire, activate, onboard, and support customers with a strong focus on customer success in order to generate predictable revenue.

Predicting Growth

How to achieve predictable revenue? Predictable high growth is not the result of just adding marketing and sales resources. Predictable growth derives from a thorough prediction process in which all departments must be involved. You analyze with your marketing and sales teams how you can predictably generate an ever-increasing number of high-quality leads that you can predict-

---

44   Predictable Revenue: Turn Your Business Into A Sales Machine With The $100 Million Best / by Aaron Ross and Marylou Tyler.

ably convert into paying key target customers. You analyze with your engineering and product teams what this entails in terms of products and product features to be developed. You discuss with your HR department what your plans mean in terms of finding and hiring the employees required to deliver on your growth plan. You focus on predicting the revenues stemming from new customers you want to predictably acquire, from the existing customer base that you aspire retaining, and from up- and cross-sells that you want to make to your highly delighted customers. Very often, and much to the surprise of many founders, the customer success team, which is in charge of retaining your customer base and up- and cross-selling, has much more revenue responsibility than your marketing and sales teams. This holds true especially the bigger your existing customer base gets.

FastScaling - On the basis of a relentless and company-wide focus on customer success, product/market-fit, product/channel-fit, strong unit economics, and a scalable technology infrastructure, efficiently and **predictably** *leading and* **scaling a** **business** *fast towards market leadership in a large market.*

There are two approaches to predicting growth that I have seen working well. You can forecast your growth on the basis of your historic performance and status quo. Alternatively, you backcast by setting clear future revenues targets and working backwards.

Forecasting

Forecasting uses historical data as input to forecast the future as output. You analyze your historic business performance in order to make reasonable assumptions about how the future may develop and how you can drive growth.

How many leads have you been able to generate per month, geography, channel, and customer segment? How has the conversion funnel been looking? How many marketing and salespeople have been required to achieve your historic growth? How much time has it taken to hire, onboard, train, and ramp up your marketing and salespeople as well as your customer success managers? What has been the workforce turnover in these departments? How much of your revenue has been derived from up- and cross-sells? Have you seen saturation in any markets, segments, or channels? There are certainly many more questions you must answer and data points you must gather depending on your target market, target customer group, and business model.

If you have answered these questions and gathered enough data points, you can start forecasting the future. Considering your constraints in terms of hiring, onboarding, training, and ramping up your workforce as well as your financing means, you can decide where growth is supposed to be coming from and how fast you want to grow.

Let us look at a fictional software-as-a-service (SaaS) company in order to see how this forecasting process could look.

The software-as-a-service (SaaS) company invests $1,000,000 each month in paid marketing and generates 10,000 leads per month. The marketing team nurtures the leads and converts them into 3,000 marketing qualified leads (MQL). The inside sales team qualifies 1,500 marketing qualified leads as sales qualified leads (SQL), and converts the sales qualified leads into 1,000 customers.

Each customer generates a monthly contribution of $100. This translates into new monthly recurring revenues (MRR) of $100,000 ($100 * 1,000 customers).

On the basis of a detailed analysis of the company's historic performance, the founders infer that they can increase the number of monthly leads to 50,000. But they also realize that their marketing and sales resources do not yet suffice to successfully generate, nurture, and convert such leads. At the same time, they are confident that they can hire, onboard, train, and ramp up the human resources needed within the next 24 months. They decide to hire accordingly and increase the money spent on paid marketing over time to $5,000,000. After 24 months, the company is supposed to generate 50,000 leads, 5,000 new customers, and $500,000 in new monthly recurring revenues.

As high growth may derive from exploiting more than one key target customer group, more than one distribution channel, and more than one target market, as well as from increasing the average revenue per existing customer, the founders must go through similar prediction processes in relation to all other revenue growth drivers. In essence, they forecast the aggregate top line growth, the workforce requirements, and all other costs associated with achieving this growth plan, especially marketing, sales, customer success, product, engineering and G&A costs. Correspondingly, they see how their EBITDA develops over time.

Increasing the investment in sales and marketing can boost top line growth and profitability in the long run. Short term, such investments may however lead to a significant increase in initial cash outflow and a corresponding financing need.[45] Therefore, forecasting must not stop at the income statement level. You must also forecast your cash flow.

Backcasting

Backcasting starts in the future with the revenue target you have and requires you to calculate backwards from there in terms of what you need to do in order to achieve your goals.

It may help you particularly in connection with the discussions you may have from time to time with your investors and board members about your company's growth targets. If investors or board members would like you to grow 100% year-on-year for the next three years, you can calculate backwards and tell your board what this means operationally and from an investment perspective.

The backcasting technique is not a short cut and not about only coming up with a monthly top line growth rate that you want to hit. If done correctly, backcasting is a process as thorough as the forecasting process. You just start at the end and calculate backwards considering your past performance and the resources you need. You also look at your income statement and your cash flow statement.

45   This is described in more depth in the Appendix.

In our example, the board of directors may ask the founders whether it would be possible to generate 10,000 new customers and $1,000,000 in new monthly recurring revenues in month 24. The founders would calculate backwards in order to understand whether this was indeed possible and, if so, what this would mean across departments and in terms of investments required.

Whether you apply forecasting or backcasting, or both, is a very subjective decision you have to make. For either approach, you will first have to analyze your historic performance as this is the basis for your assumptions going forward. On that basis you can assess how major cost, revenue, and cash drivers may develop over time. You can then either forecast or set a specific target and work backwards.

Both approaches have pros and cons. Forecasting may entail that you overemphasize your current successes, failures, and concerns as the present developments are always psychologically more present. In contrast, backcasting may lead you into the confirmation bias trap where you only see what you want to see. You may set an ambitious target and find reasons to believe that you can achieve this target.

However, both techniques can lead to satisfactory outcomes. More important than the technique is the process you go through. It is the process that matters most.

Conducting a Thorough Prediction Process

You cannot possibly know how the future will develop. You make your decisions and predictions in light of uncertainty and incomplete information. If you make a decision, like a decision to heavily fuel the growth engine, but do not achieve your predictable high growth goal, do not infer that the decision was wrong. Your decision may have been perfectly right, but unexpected external factors or just bad luck may have interfered. The opposite may be true as well. You may achieve your goal despite having made a wrong decision. Many successes have to do with luck. But you can reduce the luck part and increase the probability of generating predictable high growth by running a proper process.

In order to run a proper process, I encourage you to involve your key employees from all departments in your forecasting and backcasting processes. I also suggest you create a diverse team that provides for different views at the same problem.

As sustainable high growth is certainly an ambitious goal, you may ask your teams to be ambitious, bullish, and bold. They need to stretch. But you should also encourage objectivity, transparency, and dissenting views. Your goal is to run a process that considers any information available and goals that get the buy-in from your C-Levels and key employees.

If you have gone through the forecasting or backcasting exercise with your team and have established a business plan that is based on historic data and reasonable assumptions for the future, I suggest you do a final overall check in terms of a pre-mortem analysis.

While a post-mortem analysis looks at the past, a pre-mortem analysis looks into the future in terms of what could go wrong. Assume you fail and do not generate predictable high growth.

What could be reasons for your failure? Assemble your team and brainstorm why you may fail. The outcome of this process may help you identify blind spots and topics where you might have been overly optimistic. Write down the obstacles to achieving your goals and have your team dig deep into these topics again. Maybe, you will have to adjust your plans, maybe not.

In any case, a pre-mortem analysis can be a good final check-point and tool that allows you to double-check whether your plan is ambitious and realistic at the same time.

If you want to run a sustainable high growth business, you will have to constantly measure whether you are on track and achieve your targets. You should discuss with your team on a monthly, weekly, and daily basis what works and what does not work as well as potential reasons why you fail and how you should adapt.

· · · · ·

Predictable growth must not necessarily lead to efficient growth. But efficient growth is what you need to strive for if you want to limit your founder dilution. In the next chapter, we will discuss how to achieve high growth cash efficiently and how to measure your growth efficiency.

Key Founder Takeaways

☐ Predictable revenue is not the result of simply adding marketing and sales resources. Predictable revenue is the result of a thorough and company-wide prediction process.

☐ You analyze with your marketing and sales teams how you can predictably generate an ever-increasing number of high-quality leads that you can predictably convert into paying key target customers.

☐ You analyze with your engineering and product teams what this entails in terms of products and product features to be developed.

☐ You discuss with your HR department what your plans mean in terms of finding and hiring the employees required to deliver on your growth plan.

☐ You focus on predicting the revenues stemming from new customers you want to predictably acquire, from the existing customer base that you aspire retaining, and from up- and cross-sells that you want to make to your highly delighted customers.

☐ The prediction process must not stop at revenue, nor at EBITDA level. You must also predict your cash flow.

☐ There are two approaches to predicting revenue growth that can lead to good outcomes.

☐ Forecasting uses historical data as input to forecast the future as output. You analyze your historic business performance in order to make reasonable assumptions about how the future may develop and how you can drive growth. Considering your constraints in terms of hiring, onboarding, training, and ramping up your workforce as well as your financing means, you can decide where growth is supposed to be coming from and how fast you want to grow.

☐ Backcasting starts in the future with the revenue target you have and requires you to calculate backwards from there in terms of what you need to do in order to achieve your goals.

☐ Both approaches have pros and cons. Forecasting may entail that you overemphasize your current successes, failures, and concerns. In contrast, backcasting may lead you into the confirmation bias trap where you only see what you want to see.

☐ More important than the approach is the process that you go through.

☐ A proper process is run objectively, transparently, and encourages dissenting views. It includes key employees from all departments and team members with diverse backgrounds.

☐ A pre-mortem analysis can be a good final checkpoint and tool that allows you to double-check whether your plan is ambitious and realistic at the same time.

☐ If you want to run a sustainable high growth business, you will have to constantly measure whether you are on track and achieve your targets.

CHAPTER 11

Growing Efficiently

Money is like gasoline during a road trip. You don't want to run out of gas on your trip, but you're not doing a tour of gas stations.

TIM O'REILLY, FOUNDER AND CEO OF O'REILLY MEDIA

FastScaling is not only about high growth. FastScaling is also about achieving sustainable high growth and a massive valuation efficiently. Only if you also scale cash efficiently, you can retain a major stake in your company.

Does growing cash efficiently mean that you should not raise cash from investors at all? No, absolutely not. It means that you must grow as efficiently as possible. You need to find the right balance between growth and cash burn. You want to achieve predictable high growth without unnecessarily burning too much cash. If you FastScale you can make a deliberate decision in this regard. You can avoid being surprised by your cash burn.

Accelerating growth after having established the FastScaling foundation already leads to more efficient growth and less external cash need. Product/market fit and product/channel fit usually entail compelling unit economics and a short payback period. Focusing on customer success and running a diligent revenue, cost, and cash flow prediction process will further positively impact your growth and cash efficiency. You already scale more efficiently than companies pursuing a more aggressive approach to growth.

But you can do even better if you make growth efficiency a company-wide priority and do not follow some typical patterns of inefficient growth.

Growth Inefficiency Patterns

Growth inefficiency can have many causes. And the easiest way to avoid inefficient growth is to make growth efficiency a priority. You, as the leader, have to be the role model who leads by example with a strong tone from the top in this regard.

But there are a few patterns of inefficient growth I have noticed. Overspending on customer acquisition, hiring too many employees, and creating unnecessary complexity are three of them.

Overspending on Customer Acquisition

Strong unit economics are a good basis for accelerating growth if all other FastScaling building blocks are in place. Strong unit economics demonstrate that the value you can extract from your customers by far exceeds the costs you incur to acquire your customers. Strong unit economics are a good sign for profitable growth and a viable business model.

However, while strong unit economics provide great insights in terms of profitability, they do not tell you how much cash you need. The more you invest in customer acquisition and accelerating growth, the higher your initial cash burn will get, despite strong unit economics.[46] This holds true at least if you do not recoup your customer acquisition costs with the first customer purchase, transaction, or recurring fee paid. If you do not recoup your customer acquisition costs with the first customer purchase, you increase your initial cash outflow the more you invest in growth. I have seen founders who could not believe their eyes when they invested in growth on the basis of strong unit economics and saw their monthly cash burn going through the roof. In connection with recurring revenue businesses,

*FastScaling - On the basis of a relentless and company-wide focus on customer success, product/ market-fit, product/ channel-fit, strong unit economics, and a scalable technology infrastructure, **efficiently** and predictably leading and **scaling a business** fast towards market leadership in a large market.*

this phenomenon is described as the cash flow trough.[47] Even on the basis of strong unit economics, you incur high monthly expenses from day one, but generate cash deriving from monthly recurring fees only over a long period of time. It usually takes months until a new sales rep breaks even in terms of the relation between her salary and the recurring fees she generates.

---

46   This impact is described in more detail in the Appendix.

47   SaaS Economics – Part 1: The SaaS Cash Flow Trough / by David Skok. Retrieved from: https://www.forentrepreneurs.com/saas-economics-1/.

This phenomenon should not be of concern if you run a thorough growth prediction process as described in the previous chapter. In this process, you consider this phenomenon and carefully balance growth and cash burn. Only those founders who want to grow by simply investing in marketing and sales without planning carefully are usually struck by surprise and fall into this growth inefficiency trap of overspending on customer acquisition.

Hiring Too Many Employees Too Fast

After a fundraising process, money is in the bank account and all teams expect they can eventually hire and scale up their teams. Not only the marketing and sales teams, this applies as well to the product and engineering teams and the G&A-related departments.

Keep a close eye on your teams' hiring activities. Ensure your teams hire so you can always be FastScaling. They should hire the resources they actually need in order to achieve their targets and next milestones. But you must avoid organizational slack in the sense that you end up with more employees than you actually need. If all teams hire just a little bit more than they need, you may quickly run into significant additional and unnecessary monthly cash outflow and have to fire employees again.

Creating Unnecessary Complexity

There is another growth inefficiency pattern I have recognized at companies that are about to raise or have just raised growth capital. The founders understandably want to demonstrate they can significantly grow their businesses. But some founders lose focus. Instead of scaling the existing business and adding a growth channel, a key target customer segment, or a new target market, they want to achieve everything at the same time. They want to establish new channels and generate product/market fit with regard to new customer segments and in new markets, often expansion markets.

The problem is that the founders underestimate the complexity that comes with adding new channels, targeting new customer segments, and expanding into new markets all at the same time.

For instance, different customer segments usually have different expectations as to the product offering. What is satisfactory to the small customer segment may not be sufficient to the mid-size and enterprise customer segments. The same applies to customers active in different industries. Their needs differ. You cannot just throw the existing product at customers with different needs. You need to adjust your product offering.

Product/channel fit is difficult to find. Many startups do not get one channel to work. There are only a few that manage to successfully establish more than one channel. You cannot simply 'add' another channel. Finding another working channel through which you can access your key target customers takes much time and effort and may also require you to adjust your products.

Customers in new markets, especially international expansion markets, live in different cultures, may have slightly different needs, and may expect a different acquisition approach. Not to forget about the language obstacles that have to be overcome.

Product, tech, and go-to-market need to be adjusted to the new market characteristics. Usually, a great deal of work for your teams.

In a high growth environment, you will be confronted with many problems and complexities. Even if you want to scale your existing business 'only', you will have to overcome many obstacles. You, therefore, need to focus and prioritize. If you want to accelerate growth by targeting new customers, customer segments or markets, and adding growth channels, make deliberate team decisions in this regard. Often, it is advisable to pursue a step-by-step approach rather than an all-at-once approach. Complexity is a growth killer! Try to keep complexity at a minimum as long as possible.

Measuring Growth Efficiency

You can actually avoid falling into all growth inefficiency traps if you follow the process described in Chapter 10. Be smart and plan your growth journey thoroughly. Then measure your growth efficiency.

Measuring unit economics and your payback period is of paramount importance in order to assess whether your company has established the FastScaling foundation and has achieved high growth readiness. And you need to continue tracking your unit economics.

But measuring the unit economics and the payback period is insufficient if you want to measure your growth efficiency. One drawback of the unit economics concept in terms of measuring growth efficiency is the fact that the unit economics compare the customer lifetime value with your customer acquisition costs in terms of what you spend on marketing and sales only. It disregards what you spend on product, engineering, and G&A.

In order to measure growth efficiency, I recommend you supplement the unit economics concept and the payback period metric with additional growth efficiency metrics.

A great starting point is to compare the new business revenues you have generated in the current period with all operating expenses you have had in the previous period. This growth efficiency metric is calculated as follows:

Growth Efficiency 1 = (Revenue in Current Period - Revenue in Previous Period)/Operating Expenses in Previous Period

The Growth Efficiency 1 metric tells you how much you invest in marketing, sales, product, engineering, and G&A in order to generate new business revenue. It looks beyond marketing and sales efficiency.

At the same time, the cash Growth Efficiency 1 metric disregards your cost of goods sold (CoGS). You can adjust the Growth Efficiency metric 1 accordingly and compare gross profit with operating expenses. You calculate the Growth Efficiency 2 metric as follows:

Growth Efficiency 2 = (Gross Profit in Current Period - Gross Profit in Previous Period)/Operating Expenses in Previous Period

From here, you can get more and more granular and compare each operating expense category with revenue and gross profit growth. This will enable you to also track over time the impact your investments in certain categories have on your revenue, or gross profit growth. I suggest you definitely look at what I call the Growth Efficiency 3 metric that focuses solely on all growth-related operating expenses. It disregards G&A as a minor growth-related expense category and is calculated as follows:

Growth Efficiency 3 = (Gross Profit in Current Period - Gross Profit in Previous Period)/Marketing, Sales, Product and Engineering Costs in Previous Period

In order to assess your growth efficiency, you certainly need something to which you can compare your metrics. Look at comparable (public) companies and analyze their growth efficiency. There is plenty of publicly available data out there. However, if you cannot find the data of comparable companies, you must at least look at the development of your growth efficiency metrics over time. They should improve!

The growth efficiency metrics explained above should be relevant and provide valuable insights at each and every company. But there are certainly also business model specific metrics you may track.

To give you an example, if you pursue a software-as-a-service (SaaS) business model, you may also analyze whether you comply with the 'rule of 40'. The 'rule of 40' is a rule of thumb according to which the sum of your revenue growth rate and your profit margin should at least be 40. If you grow by 80%, you can have a negative EBITDA margin of 40%. If you want to learn not only about your growth efficiency but also about your cash efficiency, you may instead work with your free cash flow margin, and calculate the sum of the revenue growth rate and the free cash flow margin.

Look also at business model specific growth efficiency metrics!

· · · · ·

Growing efficiently is important if you want to limit your dilution deriving from raising cash in order to fuel the growth of your business. If you pursue the FastScaling approach to growing your business, you will already have come quite far in this regard. If you additionally avoid some typical inefficiency traps and constantly measure your growth efficiency, you are well on track to achieve high sustainable growth in a cash efficient manner.

Make growth and cash efficiency a guiding principle when you lead your organization through high growth and towards a massive valuation. In the next chapter, we will explore exactly this: how to successfully lead a high growth organization.

Key Founder Takeaways

☐ If you want to grow efficiently, you must find the right balance between growth and cash burn.

☐ Accelerating growth after having established the FastScaling foundation already leads to more efficient growth and less cash burn.

☐ But you can do even better if you do not follow some typical patterns of inefficient growth: overspending on customer acquisition, hiring too many employees, and creating unnecessary complexity.

☐ Unless you recoup your customer acquisition costs with the cash flow you generate from your customers' first purchase, first monthly fee, or first transaction, you will generate an initial cash outflow from any new customer you acquire. The more you invest, the higher your initial cash outflow.

☐ Keep a close eye on your teams' hiring activities, especially after a successful fundraising. Ensure your teams hire the resources they actually need in order to achieve their targets and next milestones. You must avoid organizational slack in the sense that you end up with more employees than you actually need.

☐ In a high growth environment, you will be confronted with many problems and complexities. Even if you want to scale your existing business 'only', you will have to overcome many obstacles. You therefore need to focus and prioritize. Try to keep complexity at a minimum as long as possible.

☐ You can avoid all growth inefficiency traps if you follow the process described in Chapter 10. Only the founders who blindly scale by simply adding marketing and sales resources and hiring recklessly will be surprised by unexpected cash burn. Be smart and plan your growth thoroughly.

☐ You want to understand your company's overall growth and cash efficiency. Measure the Growth Efficiency metrics 1 to 3 explained in this chapter that especially take into account cost of goods sold (CoGS) and costs other than marketing and sales costs. Additionally, keep track of company and business model specific growth and cash efficiency metrics.

☐ You should try to compare your growth efficiency with the growth efficiency of comparable companies. If you cannot find the respective data of comparable companies, you must at least look at the development of your own growth efficiency metrics. Needless to say, they should improve!

CHAPTER 12

Leading a High Growth Organization

Great teams are created by hiring talented people who are adults and want nothing more than to tackle a challenge, and then communicating to them, clearly and continuously, about what that challenge is.

PATTY MCCORD, AUTHOR OF 'POWERFUL' AND
FORMER CHIEF TALENT OFFICER AT NETFLIX

Your leadership skills can make or break your dream of building a massively valuable business.

As your business develops towards a high growth company, you continually encounter new obstacles that you have to overcome. Strong leadership skills help you successfully deal with the respective challenges.

There are many good books on leadership and I strongly encourage you to digest as many as possible. In the following four chapters, I am going to share with you my observations regarding how founders have successfully led high growth organizations, built high growth organizations, created high-functioning boards of directors, and raised growth capital.

In this chapter, we will discuss the leadership skills I have seen in successful founders. Leadership skills that you may already have, or want to acquire, and that will help you achieve your goals.

Leading by Example

Many of the strongest leaders I worked with were role models who led by example.

Leading by example has often meant doing small things like showing the right work attitude, working hard, and being present. For instance, I have been on a board of directors of a high growth business and attended a board meeting. After the board meeting had been closed, all board members left for the airport. Unfortunately, my flight got cancelled and I returned to the company office to continue working from there. When I arrived at the office at 5:30 p.m., there were only few employees present and the complete top management had already left. This company had already had Growth Efficiency problems and had especially displayed a rather low Growth Efficiency 3 index pointing towards low employee productivity. But the founders had always stressed they could not grow any leaner.

After my latest experience, I discussed this topic again with the founders and asked them to investigate how they could improve growth efficiency. Then, the Covid-19 pandemic hit. The company had to lay off a great number of employees. But such layoffs did not impact the business too much. The productivity of the entire remaining workforce just improved significantly. The founders had to realize they could have grown more cash efficiently and could have avoided significant cash burn if they had not only made growth efficiency a priority but had also led by example in terms of showing the right work attitude. If you come to work late and leave early, do not expect your employees to come early and work long hours.

*FastScaling - On the basis of a relentless and company-wide focus on customer success, product/ market-fit, product/ channel-fit, strong unit economics, and a scalable technology infrastructure, efficiently and predictably **leading** and scaling **a business** fast towards market leadership in a large market.*

Leading by example has also to do with going the extra mile and learning enough in each growth discipline. While your employees will not expect you to be an expert in all areas of expertise, they will test whether you have the skills required to ask the right questions and to guide them in what they call their area of expertise. I have worked with a CEO who had transitioned from a high strategy consultancy role into his CEO role. He was unable to make tough decisions in areas in which he was not so proficient. When growth slowed down, the CEO was faced with a situation in which the Chief Marketing Officer blamed the Chief Sales Officer for not converting high quality leads, and the Chief Sales Officer was blaming the Chief Marketing Officer for not generating high quality leads. The CEO was unable to zoom in, to understand, and resolve the issue. The issue dragged out and it took almost half a year until the board of directors figured out that the company faced a severe conversion funnel issue. Leads were not scored accurately, and high-quality leads were not nurtured properly. The marketing and sales teams were not incentivized to work cooperatively towards a joint goal. And customer success was considered a support function. We lost precious time and resources until we solved the issue. We ultimately decided to hire a coach for the CEO and a Chief Revenue Officer in order to create a state-of-the-art growth engine. As you hold this book in your hands, you are a founder who wants to be sufficiently proficient in every growth discipline. Good! This will help you lead your organization towards success.

Leading by example and being a role model also means that you walk the talk and exemplify through your own actions what you expect from the rest of the organization. If you want the whole organization to embrace the FastScaling methodology, do not judge success and incentivize your employees solely on the basis of top line growth. If customer success is your north star, live up to this and relentlessly drive your organization towards customer success. Prioritize it! Show that you want to create a viable business and demonstrate a relentless focus on establishing the FastScaling foundation before accelerating growth.

Your business has limited resources and you must make tradeoffs. Show clear prioritization and focus. Do not always prioritize rolling out new features over creating a scalable technology and repaying technical debt. Demonstrate that scalability is a priority for you! If you measure the organizational growth and cash efficiency, do not spend cash insanely yourself.

Explain to your organization what FastScaling means and live up to the methodology. Lead by example and ensure you are the role model for your organization.

Execution, Execution, Execution

Leadership is not only about setting the right strategy, but more importantly about ensuring that your organization successfully executes your strategy.

I have seen many good strategies that failed because the founders who set the strategies were not able to ensure execution. Sam Altman, the former president of Y Combinator, once rightfully stressed: "Great execution is at least ten times more important and one hundred times harder than a good idea."[48]

There are several reasons why some founders fail to execute their plans. If there is one piece of advice I want to give, it is the following: Avoid becoming the strategist sitting in an ivory tower and looking down on your employees. Yes, you need to guide the organization and set the north star. You must be the visionary and create the strategy. But you cannot only fly at 5,000 feet. As a strong leader, you must also be able to identify issues and zoom in on them. You must be able to also fly at 500 feet and even five feet where you make your hands dirty and call the shots.[49]

48   How to Start a Startup / by Sam Altman. Retrieved from: https://startupclass. samaltman.com/courses/lec01/.

49   Ian C. Woodward, Professor of Management Practice at INSEAD, wrote a great short piece about the three leadership altitudes. See: https://knowledge.insead. edu/blog/insead-blog/the-three-altitudes-of-leadership-7541.

If you want to be a strong leader, you will have to go the extra mile and gather a good understanding of your business across departments. With this understanding, you can sense if something does not seem right. And you can ask the right questions until you have educated yourself enough so you can zoom in and make the tough calls.

Your FastScaling strategy is strong and compelling, but what counts is execution.

Setting Clear Goals

Execution starts with setting clear goals and creating accountability.

The FastScaling methodology enables you to set such clear goals. Before accelerating growth, your goals must be to get to product/market fit and product/channel fit. Your goals must include establishing a secure, stable, and scalable technology and that strong unit economics reflect your growth acceleration readiness. But you cannot work with such highly qualitative goals. Product/market fit and product/channel fit are not binary and one can have very different opinions about whether or not a technology is stable, secure, and scalable. When are unit economics actually strong enough?

You need to be more granular and set clear goals for each FastScaling building block, goals that are ambitious, achievable, and measurable. Together with your leadership team, you need to define what metrics indicate that you have found product/market fit and product/channel fit, that your technology is stable, secure, and scalable, and that your unit economics can be considered strong.

While the task of setting clear goals is certainly highly dependent on your business, I have made very good experiences using the OKR methodology developed by John Doerr. In his book 'Measure What Matters',[50] he describes how to lead with OKRs. OKR stands for objectives and key results.

An objective is the broader goal you have. For instance, you could say that getting to product/market fit and product/channel fit and ensuring a secure, stable, and scalable technology, are your objectives.

The key results are the benchmarks underlying each objective and must make your progress measurable. If you wanted to measure product/market fit using the net promoter score you would have to set clear key results you want to achieve in terms of a certain net promoter score. If you wanted to set a clear goal regarding the stability of your tech infrastructure, you could look for a certain uptime percentage you want to achieve. In light of the goal to accelerate growth on the basis of strong unit economics, you would define a certain customer lifetime value to customer acquisition costs ratio and a payback period in months that you want to hit. You should set clear goals and key results for each and every FastScaling building block.

The OKR methodology does not stop at the top management level. As soon as the top level OKRs are set and communicated

50   You can learn more about the OKR concept here: https://www.whatmatters.com.

across the organization, they are broken down into team OKRs. In the net promoter score example, you would involve all relevant teams and brainstorm how you could increase the NPS, and what each department needs to accomplish in this regard by when. Each department will then break down their respective objectives into key results that the department needs to achieve. Before you kick off, you know what each department needs to achieve. If you ensure that people are responsible for specific objectives and key results you have also ensured accountability.

You are not micromanaging. You have given your employees space to be creative and find their own ways to achieve their goals. At the same time, you have been absolutely clear about what you expect. Monitor progress and adjust course if needed.

Communication, Self-Regulation, and Self-Awareness

Leading people successfully requires you to communicate well with all stakeholders involved in scaling your business. Business angels, early-stage investors, potential growth capital investors, your board of directors, your shareholders, your employees, suppliers, partners, and customers. You may encounter many conflicts of interests and divergent views and perceptions. People will carefully watch how you deal with these situations, personalities, and conflicts.

Great books have been written about what makes a strong leader, and I am not going to tell you how you should lead and which leadership style you should apply. After all, I am convinced that you have to be authentic anyway. People sense if you masquerade as someone else. But I will share with you a list of questions you may ask yourself. The questions have to do with communication, self-regulation, and self-awareness and may help you reflect on your leadership style and ability to deal with conflicts. You will have to draw your own conclusions, but I guess that me asking these questions shows you how I believe a strong leader might answer them.

- Do you manage your emotions effectively?

- Can you control your impulses and moods?

- Are you consciously communicating?

- Do you think before you speak and act?

- Do you genuinely listen, or do you listen already thinking about how to respond?

- Do you gather insights and facts before you interpret and act?

- Do you communicate effectively ensuring that your messages are well-understood?

- Do you create an environment where people feel 'safe'?

- Do you have empathy and give people space to share personal and professional views and feelings?

- Do you encourage opinion sharing, debate and fresh perspectives?

- Do you work to connect emotionally with your employees and make them feel seen, heard, and valued?

- Do you show respect?

- Do you pursue a 'tough on the issue, soft on the people' approach?

- Are you radically honest without making it personal?

- Are you aware of your strengths and weaknesses?

- Do you hire people who complement you?

- Do you appreciate diversity and hire accordingly?

- Do you hire people who have better skills than you?

- Do you hire people who can tell you what to do or people whom you can tell what to do?

- Do you give credit for successes and assume responsibility for failure?

- Do you empower people and delegate important tasks?

- Do you walk the talk?

- Are you trustworthy?

- Are you alert to confirmation bias and to searching for and interpreting information in a way it confirms your beliefs, desires, and preconceptions, and thereby to disregarding important information and deviating thoughts?

- Do you consult your key stakeholders before you make material decisions?

- Do you trade your values for value?

Leading Remote Teams

Since the Covid-19 pandemic, many companies have asked their employees to work remotely. Remote work is here to stay and creates new challenges and opportunities for leaders.

As to the challenges, remote work can lead to less personal and social interaction as well as difficulties in terms of accessing and sharing information. Some founders also fear that remote work leads to reduced employee productivity potentially deriving from distraction at home. If leaders have allowed teams to work in silos and have not ensured that diverse cross-functional teams work towards common goals, the silo issue may exacerbate.

But working remotely also provides many benefits. Eventually, remote work can reduce the company's operating expenses. Very often, expensive office space and equipment is not needed anymore. Employees need to travel less, which not only reduces travel costs but also the company's carbon footprint. Offering the opportunity to work remotely, at least partially, can also be an attractive proposition *vis-à-vis* job applicants. You may be able to attract great talent with this offering. As employees may not have to relocate anymore, you may also be able to tap into an incredibly larger pool of applicants. Being able to hire the right people can be a real competitive advantage.

Leaders must therefore proactively tackle the challenges and embrace the opportunities that come with the proliferation of remote work and videoconferencing tools like Microsoft Teams, Zoom, and Google Meet. It is not only about cost reduction and a greater pool of applicants you can access. In my experience, you can also increase employee productivity and satisfaction if you approach remote work correctly. I suggest you ask yourself the following questions:

- Have we provided our employees with the resources needed, especially in terms of technology and home office equipment?

- With this equipment, can our employees access and share relevant information?

- Are we flexible enough and encourage both work from home and in the office?

- Have we set clear rules so that our employees know what we expect?

- Do we lead and manage towards goal achievement or do we micromanage?

- Do we trust our employees?

- Do we encourage and implement daily, weekly, and monthly check-in calls, and do we check-in often enough with our key employees?

- Do we make sure that communication takes place, both social and work related?

- Do we encourage social interactions?

Certainly, this list is not exhaustive. Listen to what your employees tell you about what they expect, need, and suggest in order to make remote work a competitive advantage for your company. Be proactive, listen and lead. This may lead to a fully remote or hybrid work environment. There is no right or wrong. You need to find what works for you.

· · · · ·

If you have or acquire strong leadership skills, set clear goals, lead by example with a strong focus on execution, and embrace the opportunities deriving from the proliferation of remote work, you are well-positioned to lead a high growth organization towards success. We discuss how to establish a high growth organization in the next chapter.

Key Founder Takeaways

☐ As your business develops towards a high growth company, you will consistently encounter new obstacles that you have to overcome. Strong leadership skills will help you successfully deal with the respective challenges.

☐ I encourage you to be a role model and a leader who leads by example.

☐ This means doing supposedly small things like showing the right work attitude, working hard, and being present. It also means that you walk the talk and exemplify through your own actions what you expect from the rest of the organization.

☐ Leading by example also means going the extra mile and learning enough in each growth discipline. While your employees will not expect you to be an expert in all areas of expertise, they will test whether you have the skills required to ask the right questions and to guide them in what they call their area of expertise.

☐ Explain to your organization what FastScaling means and live up to the methodology. First validate the fundamental elements of your business model, then fuel the growth engine and FastScale.

☐ Set clear goals for each and every FastScaling building block, goals that are ambitious, achievable, and measurable.

☐ What differentiates strong leaders from their weaker peers is often their ability to execute on the strategy.

☐ Leading people successfully requires you to communicate well with all stakeholders involved in scaling your business. Reflect on your leadership style and ability to deal with conflicts. Are you self-aware, self-regulated and consciously communicating well?

☐ You should proactively tackle the challenges and embrace the opportunities that come with the proliferation of remote work. You may be able to attract great talent with this offering. As employees may not have to relocate anymore, you may also be able to tap into an incredibly larger pool of applicants. You may reduce operating expenses and increase employee productivity and satisfaction.

CHAPTER 13

Building a High Growth Organization

Startups should not have growth teams. The whole company should be the growth team.[51]

AXEL SCHULTZ, VP PRODUCT GROWTH AT FACEBOOK

The employees and the flat organizational structure that work well in times where you strongly focus on getting to product/market fit and product/channel fit are likely not the ideal employees and organizational structure that you need when you heavily fuel the growth engine and FastScale.

In fact, on your journey, you will have to hire and say goodbye to many good employees and to constantly adjust your organizational set-up.

Hiring People Who Tell You 'What' and 'How'

In fact, change is the only constant when it comes to the right organizational set up for achieving predictable high growth. It is

---

51   Retrieved from: https://startupclass.samaltman.com/courses/lec06/.

your leadership responsibility to build and adjust your organization accordingly.

In this regard, I share with Jim Collins the most important aspect is *who* you hire. Hire the right people and they will tell you the 'What' and the 'How'. In his book, 'Good to Great', he said:

"You are a bus driver. The bus, your company, is at a standstill, and it's your job to get it going. You have to decide where you're going, how you're going to get there, and who's going with you. Most people assume that great bus drivers immediately start the journey by announcing to the people on the bus where they're going - by setting a new direction or by articulating a fresh corporate vision. In fact, leaders of companies that go from good to great start not with 'where' but with 'who'. They start by getting the right people on the bus, the wrong people off the bus, and the right people in the right seats. And they stick with that discipline - first the people, then the direction - no matter how dire the circumstances." [52]

In this chapter, I consequently focus on some key positions that you may want to fill at your company in order to achieve your high growth plans. If you hire the right people, you can jointly define how you want to go about achieving your goals pursuing the FastScaling approach.

---

52   Good To Great: Why Some Companies Make the Leap... and Others Don't / by Jim Collins.

I will talk about many C-Level roles.[53] If you are a founder of an early-stage company, you may not be able to afford to have all these positions filled. In such case, you must prioritize. Unfortunately, I cannot give you clear guidance on relative priority and when to hire which of these senior roles. For instance, if you yourself have a strong tech background or a strong tech co-founder you may not immediately need to hire a Chief Technology Officer. If your marketing, sales, and customer success teams nicely cooperate and deliver on your growth plans, you may not need a Chief Revenue

*FastScaling - On the basis of a relentless and company-wide focus on customer success, product/market-fit, product/channel-fit, strong unit economics, and a scalable technology infrastructure, efficiently and predictably **leading** and scaling a **business** fast towards market leadership in a large market.*

Officer. It all depends. I suggest you look at all FastScaling building blocks and decide which roles to prioritize.

It is all about establishing a diverse and complementary team that embraces the FastScaling strategy and successfully cooperates and works together towards achieving the clear goals you set. You must have people who execute.

If I had to prioritize, anyway, I would recommend you hire a

---

53   Whether you hire at C level or at VP level needs to be decided on a company-by-company and stage-by-stage basis.

Chief People Officer sooner than later, and hire a Chief Operating Officer only when you are convinced that you cannot successfully lead the organization any longer without having a second in command.

Chief Technology Officer & Chief Product Officer

If you want to make your customers incredibly successful, your customer must have a great customer experience and a great return on investment. The quality of your products and services matter as much as the quality of the underlying technology.

You therefore need a strong Chief Product Officer (CPO) who focuses on product and ensures that the product solves your customers' pains conveniently. And you need an outstanding Chief Technology Officer (CTO) who ensures the respective products and product features are being developed as well as technology stability, security, and scalability.

Some companies combine these roles and put product and technology under one person. And as the Chief Technology Officer and the Chief Product Officer share the ultimate goal of making the customer happier, this often works well in the earlier days of a company when the product is not very complex and when you focus on getting to product/market fit and product/channel fit.

But in my experience, it is advisable to separate the roles and have both a Chief Product Officer and a Chief Technology Officer, at the latest when you want to enter the FastScaling high growth phase.

The Chief Product Officer can solely focus on the product and your customers. She can ensure that the product roadmap is closely aligned with your key target customers' needs and expectations. The Chief Technology Officer can concentrate on delivering on the product road map and ensuring technology stability, security, and scalability.

Sometimes, tension arises between the Chief Product Officer and the Chief Technology Officer. While the Chief Product Officer requests the development of specific products and product features, the Chief Technology Officer wants to focus on repaying technical debt and improving the stability, security, and scalability of the technology infrastructure. This tension is actually good as long as you successfully orchestrate your leadership team towards a well-functioning system of checks and balances. The tension can ultimately lead to a good prioritization of value adding products and product features and a sufficient focus on the technology infrastructure.

Your Chief Product Officer and your Chief Technology Officer have strong impact on customer success, your overall business performance, and your ability to achieve your predictable high growth plans. Make sure they work well together as a team. If tension arises, zoom in and help them solve the issue.

Chief Marketing Officer, Chief Sales Officer & Chief Customer Success Officer

Many startups get to initial traction and generate between

$1m and $5m in revenue but have a hard time getting through the growth valley of death. They have difficulties scaling the business to $50m and $100m in revenue. This can have many causes. And this whole book is about how to avoid typical growth-related mistakes and getting through the growth valley of death. But hiring the wrong people for your marketing, sales, and customer success teams is certainly one root cause for failure.

On the one hand, you want to hire people who tell you what to do. On the other hand, people tend to do at the new company what worked at their former company. But, in fact, this may not be the right go-to-market and customer success strategy at your company. I encourage you to focus your interviews on this area of tension. You need to identify the talent who comes with great leadership skills enabling her to successfully lead teams and who is able to adapt to the FastScaling growth strategy at your company.

As a board member, I have been involved in many searches for respective talents. Based on this experience, I can give you the following guidance:

Do not believe that hiring people from big corporations always does the trick. Someone who has led teams of hundreds of people at big corporations must not be the right hire for your company.

You need growth experts who fit the growth stage you are in.

Look for people who understand your go-to-market and customer success philosophy and embrace your company-wide focus on customer success.

Look for people who embrace a compensation system that includes company-wide bonus factors.

Make sure you hire someone who knows what works and, at the same time, is open to experimenting and figuring out why your company is different.

Make sure that the candidate is open to hiring the right people for your business and not only people she worked with at her previous company.

Chief Revenue Officer

A Chief Revenue Officer (CRO) assumes the responsibility not only over the sales team, but over all revenue-generating activities, especially marketing, sales, and customer success. She is supposed to guide these departments - in close collaboration with your Chief Product Officer (CPO) and your Chief Technology Officer (CTO) - towards the common goals of predictable high-quality lead generation, predictable conversion rates, predictable revenue, and eventually customer success.

Your Chief Revenue Officer may have in-depth knowledge and experience as to leading a certain customer-facing function. But more importantly, she should have a brilliant general understanding of all revenue-generating activities coupled with strong leadership qualities. Ultimately, she needs to be able to lead cross-functional teams.

While I have generally seen many companies thrive that have put marketing, sales, and customer success under the leadership of a strong Chief Revenue Officer, you should definitely consider hiring a Chief Revenue Officer if you encounter situations similar to the one described in the previous chapter and in which marketing, sales, and customer success teams blame each other or the product and tech teams for the poor growth performance. If you face this situation you must react fast and solve the underlying issue. You may also take on the interim Chief Revenue Officer role until you can hire an outstanding candidate for this role.

Chief Operating Officer & Chief Finance Officer

Establishing the FastScaling foundation and FastScaling your company will be challenging. FastScaling is more than refining a strategy. You must dive deep into operational, technological, and financial topics and execute on your strategy. While you are dealing with the respective challenges, business operations need to continue. Processes need to be improved and adjusted. The recruiting infrastructure needs to be aligned to the new high growth pace. Corporate governance compliance is a must. A good high growth culture in the executive team and the whole organization must be retained and shaped. KPIs must be tracked and potentially improved. The list goes on. There are two executive team members who can help you successfully cope with all these challenges at the same time, the Chief Operating Officer (COO) and the Chief Finance Officer (CFO).

Hiring a Chief Operating Officer as a second in command can enable you to focus on the most important tasks while the Chief Operating Officer ensures that your business continues to thrive. If you envisage hiring a Chief Operating Officer, make sure that the respective person embraces his role in the 'second' row. You really want someone who is highly skilled and has great leadership skills, but at the same time does not need to be in the spotlight all the time.

The Chief Finance Officer can help you steer the business on the basis of all relevant key performance indicators (KPIs) and impress investors with state-of-the-art financial documentation. When hiring a Chief Finance Officer, look for someone who not only excels at understanding your business model and its key success factor. Look for someone who is mature enough to challenge you. You want to have fruitful discussions with your Chief Finance Officer and not only an internal reporting function.

Chief People Officer

In the fast-paced environment of a high growth company, a Chief People Officer (CPO) plays a vital role.

Once you fuel your growth engine, the recruitment pace will accelerate. Your organization will be growing faster and you will have to overcome more and more people obstacles. Your company will turn from a company where everybody knows each other into a company where you, as the founder, run into employees you have never seen before.

Entering the high growth phase may also entail switching from being very frugal spending money to spending a lot of cash. The level of risk the executive team takes on is often much different from the risk it has been taking on before. The offices may look differently, too. The company may have to move offices frequently.

Employees may work remotely. Teams may be spread across floors, offices, geographies, and time zones.

HR functions are very often the last functions founders think of adding. But it is grossly negligent to enter the high growth phase without having someone in charge of sustaining the company culture and ensuring that hiring, onboarding, and training as well as organizational and people development are done in a proactive and predictable manner. The opportunity costs are high.

Just look back into Chapter 10, in which we discussed how to predict your growth going forward. Achieving your high growth plans requires you to hire many resources across your organization. If you do not hire, onboard, train, and retain great talents and ensure a great high growth culture, you will fail and not achieve your goals.

I therefore encourage you to add a VP of People or a Chief People Officer to the executive team early on.

Hiring Predictably

You must not be reactive when it comes to hiring. You need to proactively tackle this topic if you want to hire in accordance with your high growth predictions and plans. Your Chief People Officer will know this. She will have her own approach. However, you, as the founder, should also have a certain idea about how you want to go about generating a predictable and never-ending stream of strong talents with adequate skills wanting to work for you.

Working with External Agencies

I have met founders who have worked extensively with external agencies. But using external agencies is a costly endeavor, especially if you want to fill many positions. Moreover, if you consult these agencies you can never be sure whether you get to see all promising talents they identify. It might be the case that your competitor also works with the same agency and pays the agency more than you do. To whom do you think the agency will express preference?

Given this risk and the costs associated with working with external service providers, you may consider pursuing a balanced approach to working with external recruitment agencies. While it can make tremendous sense to use external reputable search firms for finding suitable C-level executives or specific hires, you may generally create a strong in-house recruitment team that proactively works on filling all other positions.

Building an In-House Recruiting Agency

Great advice comes in this regard from Mark Roberge who, in his book, 'The Sales Acceleration Formula'[54] suggests building a recruiting agency within the company. By building an internal recruitment agency, you can indeed get the best of both worlds, external agencies, and traditional in-house recruiters.

The difference between traditional in-house recruiters and an internal recruitment agency is that the employees of the latter are

---

54   The Sales Acceleration Formula : using data, technology, and inbound selling to
       go from $0 to $100 million / by Mark Roberge.

paid like external agents. They get rather moderate base salaries combined with meaningful performance bonuses. The performance bonuses are based on their fill rates as well as the timing and long-term success of their hires. They operate like external agencies. They source most of the candidates passively. They do much cold outreach and networking. And they know the company-specifics and candidate requirements by heart. They know the growth predictions and the underlying hiring needs. They can plan accordingly, long-term, and proactively, and will show you all promising candidates.

Compensating & Incentivizing

If you compensate your product, development, marketing, sales, and customer success teams based on the achievement of department-specific goals, the likelihood is high that your teams work in silos and that the company misses its growth targets.

Let us look at an example of a company that I have worked with and that experienced comparatively high early churn, high support costs, and an increasing number of bad reviews. Customer lifetime value and customer acquisition costs were deteriorating. When looking into the potential root causes, we identified the sales team was incentivized solely on the basis of deals won in the sense of customers acquired. The sales team over-promised to customers what the product could do and essentially pushed the company's products into the market. As the customers' actual return on investment fell short of the promised return on investment, the customers needed more support (costs!), churned fast (lower CLV!), and spread bad reviews (higher CAC!). We could solve this issue by adjusting the incentive system and additionally including customer success metrics into bonus factors at almost all departments. We particularly tackled the issues identified by linking bonuses to the development of early churn and retention rate as well as usage, engagement, and net promoter score results. This change had many effects, but most importantly it led to a significantly stronger focus on attracting and converting leads to key target customers and excluding non-key target customers at the top of the funnel. Marketing and sales teams did not have to nurture leads with a relatively low conversion likelihood. They did not have to over-promise anymore and the customers acquired experienced a great return on investment. The products solved the key target customers' problems in a convenient way. Great customer experience.

I am, therefore, a huge fan of supplementing department-specific goals with team and company-wide goals. Incentivize your teams on the basis of the FastScaling building blocks considering whether you are still in the process of establishing the FastScaling foundation or are already FastScaling. Customer success should always be an important incentive component.

When you suggest that all teams will be incentivized also on the basis of company-wide goals, be sure to hear thousands of arguments why this is not a good idea. Very often you will hear that employees cannot fully impact their own destiny anymore. But be persistent. You certainly need to come up with a wise combination of incentives. But if you want to steer your company towards establishing the FastScaling foundation and FastScale, corresponding company-wide incentives will encourage cross-functional team building and striving for common goals.

● ● ● ● ●

You are not alone when it comes to hiring. You can discuss all material decisions with your board of directors. You can tap into the respective knowledge of people who have seen what works and what does not. A prerequisite certainly is that you establish a high-functioning board of directors. This is the topic of the next chapter.

Key Founder Takeaways

☐ As a leader, you are responsible for adjusting your organizational set-up over and over again. The most important aspect in this regard is *who* you hire. Hire the right people and they will tell you the 'What' and the 'How'.

☐ Consider hiring a strong Chief Product Officer (CPO) who focuses on the product and ensures that the product solves your customers' pains conveniently. Think about attracting an outstanding Chief Technology Officer (CTO) who ensures technology stability, security, and scalability.

☐ If tension arises between the Chief Product Officer and the Chief Technology Officer with respect to prioritizing product development or technology scalability, orchestrate them towards a well-functioning system of checks and balances. The tension can ultimately lead to a good prioritization of value adding products and product features and a sufficient focus on the scalability of your technology infrastructure.

☐ A Chief Revenue Officer (CRO) can always be a good hire if you want to put all revenue-generating activities under one responsible person. You should definitely consider hiring a Chief Revenue Officer if you encounter situations in which marketing, sales, and customer success teams blame each other or the product and tech teams for the poor growth performance.

☐ Hiring a Chief Operating Officer (COO) as a second in command can make sense in order to enable you to focus on the most important tasks while the Chief Operating Officer ensures that your business continues to thrive.

☐ When you hire a Chief Finance Officer (CFO), look for someone who is mature enough to challenge you. You want to have fruitful discussions and not only an internal reporting function.

☐ It is grossly negligent to enter a high growth phase without having someone in charge of people and culture. The opportunity costs are high. Hiring a VP of People or a Chief People Officer (CPO) early on can be a very smart move.

☐ You should consider creating a strong in-house recruitment team that proactively works on filling open positions. You may also consider creating a recruitment agency within your company. You may be able to get the best of both worlds, an inhouse team and a recruitment agency.

☐ Supplementing department-specific goals with team

and company-wide goals may encourage your teams to jointly work on achieving common goals and to avoid working in silos. Consider incentivizing them on the basis of the FastScaling building blocks considering whether you are still establishing the FastScaling foundation or are already FastScaling.

☐ You should discuss all material organizational and people-related topics with your board of directors. You can tap into the respective knowledge of people who have seen what works and what does not.

CHAPTER 14

Creating a High-Functioning Board of Directors

Social capital, or 'networks of trust', are rooted in relationships based on a common set of norms and values that bind a group of individuals together and enable them to collaborate more effectively. Networks of trust are critical in complex systems that demand high performance under fast-paced, ambiguous, and evolving conditions. Successful outcomes in military special forces, modern aviation, championship sports, and hyper-growth startups all require teamwork that is grounded in trust and a shared sense of purpose.[55]

BRAD FELD, CO-FOUNDER OF FOUNDRY GROUP AND

TECHSTARS

Together, with your leadership team, you are in charge of conducting the day-to-day business. But you are not alone; you have your board of directors.

---

55   The Startup Community Way: Evolving an Entrepreneurial Ecosystem / by Brad Feld and Ian Hathaway.

The role of the board of directors is first and foremost to help you make material business and strategic decisions. Such decisions may include to accelerate growth, target additional customer groups and segments, add growth channels, expand into new markets, and make key hiring decisions.

*FastScaling - On the basis of a relentless and company-wide focus on customer success, product/ market-fit, product/ channel-fit, strong unit economics, and a scalable technology infrastructure, efficiently and predictably **leading** and scaling **a business** fast towards market leadership in a large market.*

Given the fact that you make material decisions within the board of directors, you must ensure you establish a high-functioning board of directors consisting of highly experienced and well-connected board members. As a high-functioning board of directors can help you achieve your high growth plans, a low-functioning board of directors can bring your growth journey to a stall.

Let us shortly recap the board governance before we dive into how to establish a high-functioning board of directors.

Board Governance Recap

Not every startup has a board of directors. Especially early-stage companies that have not yet raised capital from institutional investors often decide not to establish a formal board of directors. They work closely with their business angels who usually invest in pre-seed and seed rounds. A board of directors is normally established in connection with the first fundraising round in which a venture capital firm invests a significant amount of money in the company.

Board of Directors

The founders and major shareholders, like the investors who have invested a significant amount of money in the company, nominate the board of directors. The board directors are entitled to vote in board meetings.

While the founders tend to nominate themselves, the investors usually nominate the partner of the venture capital firm leading the deal as a board director as well as often a junior investor as a board observer.

An early-stage company usually has three to five board directors and a late-stage company can sometimes have up to and even more than nine board directors. There are divergent views as to whether a board of directors with more than five board directors can actually be a well-functioning board at all. Major concerns are around convening everyone and decision-making. While I agree that managing a board of directors with more than five board members can get difficult, I recommend you analyze on a case-by-case basis which board members really create value for your company and help you achieve your milestones. If you have committed and value-creating board members with diverse backgrounds and skills, keep them! In my experience, it usually pays off and is worth the effort.

As you will spend a significant amount of time with your board directors and since leading a high growth business can be a roller-coaster ride, you need to have people around you with whom you feel at ease. Both professional and personal fit are important when it comes to choosing your investors who ultimately nominate board directors.

Board Observer

Investors often ask for a board observer seat for their analyst or associate – in addition to a board director seat for themselves. A board observer is someone entitled to participate in board meetings without having a right to vote and sometimes even without a right to speak. In the latter case, the role is indeed essentially reduced to a mere right to be present.

While each board observer seat increases the number of people involved, granting board observer seats can make a great deal of sense from a value creation perspective. Junior investors not only help their partners prepare meetings; they can have valuable detailed knowledge on specific topics and can take on specific tasks deriving from board discussions and decisions.

If your investors ask for a board observer seat, be open. But make clear that you also expect board observers to create value.

Independent Board Members

Independent board members are very often added to the board if investors and founders cannot agree on who should have the majority on the board of directors, the founders, or the investors. In such case, the independent board member is supposed to add the required independence in decision-making.

But adding an independent board member can make sense anyway if the respective person brings something special to the table, e.g. industry knowledge, network, or commitment to mentor the founders. Irrespective of why independent board members are supposed to be added to your board of directors, always look out for experienced people who can add value and are committed to closely working with the company and you, personally.

Voting

What is being discussed controversially in the board of directors is rarely decided by voting. Normally, voting takes place after the board has formed its view and only if the share-holders' agreement or the articles of association require a formal decision.

The board of directors should not be about voting. It should be about sharing knowledge, experience, and opinions. If topics are being discussed controversially, this is actually a good sign. It shows that the board members actively engage and that you can tap into the collective knowledge of your board of directors in addition to the knowledge of the individual board members. You should thus appreciate divergent viewpoints and establish an environment that encourages fruitful open discussions.

Creating Trust

If you have found the right board governance and want to encourage fruitful discussions in which divergent viewpoints are openly shared, you need to create a trust building environment. You need to facilitate trust between you as the founder on the one hand and all other board members on the other hand as well as among the board members nominated by the investors.

In an environment determined by trust, you do not hesitate to ask for advice. You do not have to fear that asking for help is considered a sign of weakness. Investors feel comfortable dividing responsibilities and working constructively together irrespective of divergent views. They can articulate openly what is good, what is bad, and what needs to be changed or improved. Be it how meetings are prepared, how meetings are conducted, or how communication takes place.

While you cannot command your board members to trust each other, you can facilitate trust building. Trust building begins with you. You yourself can be integral. You can be authentic, honest, reliable, and transparent. You can communicate openly, walk the talk, and execute on promises made. You can be empathic and appreciate your fellow board members with all their peculiarities and different positions and interests. And you can build trust by trusting your board members first.

You can also facilitate the creation of meaningful relationships and trust among all board members before, during, and after board meetings. Regular in person meetings and dinners outside official board meetings can already bring you quite far in this regard.

Trust is hard to build, easy to break, and difficult to repair. Do not let anybody break trust. Be especially alert if you see someone trying to trade values for value. Self-optimization is a trust killer. You want to be successful together with your board members and investors. Certainly, this goes both ways.

I have experienced myself how a founder destroyed trust over and over again. I should have known. Before I signed the investment agreement, the founder wanted to deviate from what had been agreed in the term sheet. When I stressed that I always walked the talk and considered a term sheet binding from a psychological and ethical perspective, he finally agreed to implementing the term sheet. But trust was already crumbling. During board meetings, the founder listened to investor feedback, guidance, and value-creating ideas, but rarely executed anything but what he had suggested in the first place. Could we trust that he was on a joint journey with us? In connection with the next financing round, he again wanted to make last minute changes to the liquidation preference section of the shareholders' agreement. He wanted to optimize his own position to the detriment of certain investors who had already been backing him for a while. Now, trust was severely damaged. The founder continued starting his e-mails with 'Dear Team', but it never felt authentic anymore. I am strongly convinced the company could have grown even more and especially more efficiently if the founder had listened to the advice of the board of directors. An environment of trust could have boosted the growth trajectory. But once broken, you can hardly repair trust. Be trustworthy and do not trade values for value. You will get a lot back in return.

Conducting Board Meetings

Scheduling Board Meetings

Board meeting preparation starts with scheduling the meetings. Typically, board meetings are scheduled on a bi-monthly basis, but this certainly depends on the stage of your company and the specific situation you are in. Align your board meeting schedule with the internal company reporting so that you can provide the board of directors with actual numbers. For instance, you should not schedule your meetings so they take place at the very beginning of the month if you know that actual numbers cannot usually be shared until later in the month. Remember: Investors want to help, and, for this, they need to understand how the company is currently trading.

Board Material

Board members expect to receive the preparation material at least four to five business days in advance. No last-minute decks, no excuses, no whining. If something material occurs after the material has been sent out, updates are fine.

The board material should focus on the essentials and set the scene for a lively and fruitful board discussion. There is no need to create a fifty to sixty slide power point presentation. The opposite is true. Be short and precise and focus on what really matters.

A good agenda could look as follows:

- The good, the bad and the ugly (15 Minutes)

- Update on key developments, metrics, and trends (30 Minutes)

- Major topic 1 (60 Minutes)

- Major topic 2 (60 Minutes)

- Major topic 3 (60 Minutes)

- Formalities (15 Minutes)

- Closing executive session (board members and CEO/ founders only) (15-30 Minutes)

- Closing session (board members without CEO/founders) (15 Minutes)

Board meetings are not reporting or status update meetings. Nothing frustrates investors more than sitting in a room listening for hours how management goes through slides reporting on how the business is trading. Reporting should be done on a regular basis outside the board meetings so that the board members know the latest numbers and are always up to date in this regard. In board meetings, only a limited amount of time should be spent on reporting and only on the really relevant aspects.

If you get feedback on your reporting, embrace it. For instance, I have once requested that the growth efficiency metrics we discussed in Chapter 11 be added to the key performance indicator section of the reporting file. They were added but in one of the following board meetings I had to realize that this was it. They had been added. The goal was certainly not to just have another number popping up in the reporting file. The goal was to have the management team dig deeper into why the growth efficiency was not as good as it should have been. For this, they should have compared the numbers with those of comparable companies and analyzed on a granular level the key components of the metrics in order to figure out what needed improvement.

Conducting the Board Meeting

In the actual board meeting, follow the agenda and create an atmosphere that allows you to source as much input as you can from your fellow board members. This links back to the requirement to build trust and proactively ask for sharing viewpoints and advice.

It is important to keep in mind that this can also mean the board criticizes how you run the business. Take criticism as what it should be. Feedback. Feedback given by trusted advisors who want to help you improve the business. There is no sense in becoming defensive. Accept and embrace the feedback and consider any feedback valuable. If all board members share the same criticism, it may very well be grounded. If the board members have different opinions on the respective matter, listen carefully to what each board member has to say. Use the divergent feedback to make your own assessment and guide the board of directors towards a constructive dialogue that does not always have to lead to a unanimous point of view. Conflicting thoughts are the reflection of a diverse group of people with different backgrounds, knowledge, and experience. Appreciate having access to this medium.

And give feedback, too. Board members want to create value and any feedback they get on how they are doing in this regard enables them to improve.

I recommend you take minutes. Minutes not only reflect the formal decisions taken but also the information you are supposed to provide to the board members after the meeting.

Communicating Outside Board Meetings

Board members appreciate being updated outside board meetings on how the business is generally doing and on any major developments.

Find a natural rhythm for such updates. A good starting point are monthly reporting updates in which current trading and key performance indicators (KPIs) are shared. Together with such updates, you may reflect in a short and precise e-mail on the overall situation, major achievements, and challenges.

If anything material has occurred, do not wait until the next board meeting. Material information must be shared immediately. And you can always reach out to your board members and ask for help and advice. The responsibility of each board member is to create value for your business. This includes being available and responsive.

• • • • •

You are not alone. Your board members are there to help you. They are also constantly involved in fundraising processes. They know the Dos and Don'ts in this regard. Use your board of directors when you consider raising growth capital. The board of directors will help you time, prepare, and implement your fundraising process. We discuss how to raise growth capital in the next chapter.

Key Founder Takeaways

☐ Together with your leadership team, you are in charge of conducting the day-to-day business. The role of the board of directors is first and foremost to help you make material business and strategic decisions.

☐ You must ensure that you establish a high-functioning board of directors consisting of highly experienced and well-connected board members. As a high-functioning board of directors can help you achieve your high growth plans, a low-functioning board of directors can bring your growth journey to a stall.

☐ Leading a high growth business can be a roller-coaster ride. You need to have people around with whom you feel at ease. Both professional and personal fit are important when it comes to choosing your board members.

☐ The board of directors is not about voting. It is about sharing knowledge, experience, and opinions and eventually about value creation.

☐ If you have found the right board governance and want to encourage fruitful discussions in which divergent viewpoints are openly shared, you need to create trust in the board.

☐ Trust is hard to build, easy to break, and difficult to repair. Do not let anybody break trust. Be especially alert if you see someone trying to trade values for value. Self-optimization is a severe trust killer.

☐ The board material should be circulated not later than four to five business days before the actual meeting. The material should be short and precise and focus on what really matters.

☐ In board meetings, only a limited amount of time should be spent on reporting and only on the really relevant aspects.

☐ Follow the agenda and create an atmosphere that allows you to source as much input as you can from your board members. Embrace feedback, both positive and negative. Do not get defensive. Board members want to help.

☐ If anything material has occurred, do not wait until the next board meeting. Material information must be shared immediately.

☐ You can always reach out to your board members and ask for help and advice. The responsibility of each board member is to create value for your business. This includes being available and responsive.

CHAPTER 15

Raising Growth Capital

For some reason founders get their ego involved in fundraising where it's a personal victory. It is the tiniest step on the way.[56]

RON CONWAY, ANGEL INVESTOR

Pursuing the FastScaling approach to growing your business enables you to grow your business fast, predictably, and efficiently.

But growing your business efficiently does not mean you should run your business cash flow positive and never raise capital from investors. In fact, if you have established the FastScaling foundation, it can make a great deal of sense to raise capital in order to heavily fuel the growth engine and capture market share fast. If you have thoroughly gone through the prediction process described in Chapter 10, you understand how much money you have to raise in order to achieve your growth plans. And you can adjust your growth plans in order to reduce your cash burn and cash need. FastScaling enables you to find the right balance

---

56 How to Start a Startup – How to Raise Money / by Sam Altman, Ron Conway and Parker Conrad. Retrieved from: https://startupclass.samaltman.com/courses/lec09/.

between cash burn and growth. But you usually still need to raise cash from investors. In this chapter, we therefore look at how to establish a compelling pitch deck, which investors to approach, and what company valuation to accept.

Founders who want to raise growth capital are sometimes surprised by the data points growth capital investors expect to see. In fact, raising growth capital is very different from raising early-stage venture capital. Growth capital investors will expect to see all sorts of numbers and metrics and will carefully review your past performance and predictions for the future in order to validate you are running a viable business model and a company that has the potential to become the market leader in an incredibly large market.

*FastScaling - On the basis of a relentless and company-wide focus on customer success, product/market-fit, product/channel-fit, strong unit economics, and a scalable technology infrastructure, efficiently and predictably **leading** and scaling **a business** fast towards market leadership in a large market.*

Approaching Investors

I encourage you to discuss with your board of directors a short-list of investors you should approach. The potential investors need to fit your company and investment stage profile. Preferably based on previous interactions you have had with them, you are also convinced that the respective partner of the venture capital firm could add value to your board of directors. Choose your investors and board members wisely. This is, in my subjective view, more important than brand and valuation. As Mark Suster pointed out: "There is no divorce clause for founders and investors."[57]

Creating a Compelling Growth Capital Pitch Deck

If you want to raise growth capital, you need to put yourself into the shoes of your potential growth capital investors and create a pitch deck tailored to their specific interest. Ultimately, their interest is to make abnormal later stage fund returns. As a rule of thumb, but certainly different from investor to investor, they aim at making three to five times their money invested. If a growth capital investor invests $20m, you can expect that they want to achieve a return between $60m and $100m. And do not forget to consider dilution deriving from further financing rounds. For instance, if a growth capital investor invested $20m and owned 20% of your company after the financing round, which would translate into a $80m pre-money valuation and a $100m post-money valuation, you would have to sell your company for $500m if the investor expects to make five times the money invested (20% * $500m = $100m = 5 * $20m). But if you had to raise more capital before you exit the company and if your investor's shareholding was diluted to 15%, you would have to sell the company for approx. $666m ($666m * 15% = approx. 100m = 5 * $20m).

57   There's No Divorce Clause for Founders and VCs. By Mark Suster. Retrieved from: https://www.youtube.com/watch?v=ybpZMkcm9eM.

While the pitch deck should describe, in a compelling way, why investing in your company is the right thing to do, you should keep in mind that investors look for founders they can trust and with whom they can build a long and fruitful relationship. You must therefore refrain from overstating important business aspects and focus on establishing credibility by providing a visionary, but authentic, transparent, true, and fair view of your business. Be ambitious, but realistic.

Keep your deck short and precise. Make sure your slides and especially the action titles of your slides tell a consistent story.

The Executive Summary

Whether or not a pitch deck should have an executive summary slide is a matter of opinion. I personally like such introductory slides that work as a teaser and summarize the content in a very short, simple, and precise manner. Content-wise, the slide should really concentrate on what you believe the investor should be made aware of before going through the pitch deck.

Product/Market Fit

You may then explain the problem your key target customers have. Investors want to see that you solve a significant problem, preferably one that is hard to solve. Your key target customers should be in 'extreme pain'. Investors often talk about whether a product is a vitamin (nice to have) or a pain killer (must have). Just like in a drug store, vitamins are usually optional and priced lower than pain killers people buy in order to make immediate health problems disappear. Investors look for companies that sell pain killers.

The pitch deck should explain how your products and services solve your key target customers' problems and how your products and services are different from existing offerings.

As you want to raise growth capital, demonstrate that you have found product/market fit and how you measure product/market fit. You may also want to explain your vision regarding how the product is supposed to look like in 9-24 months (Product Road Map).

Product/Channel Fit

In the go-to-market section of the pitch deck, you can show which channels you use to acquire your customers and that you have found product/channel fit. You may also already touch upon your customer acquisition costs in each channel.

Technology

Good investors know that the quality of the technology can make or break the growth plans of the most promising teams and companies. Make sure you can clearly articulate your technology is stable, secure, and scalable. Show the corresponding metrics, not the names of the technologies, languages, and third-party providers you use.

Unit Economics

If, and to the extent, you have not included your unit economics into the slides dealing with product/market fit and product/channel fit, show them here and explain why and how they demonstrate your growth acceleration readiness.

Use the standard methodologies and do not artificially inflate your unit economics. I have seen founders stating their customer lifetime value to customer acquisition costs ratio will be three within the next six months. What the investors hear is: "Our actual unit economics are not good yet." If you want to or have to describe how your unit economics will look like in the future, you need to guide the reader from the current situation to the future situation. Where are you now and how will you get to the future numbers.

Market Size

The slides dealing with market size, structure, and dynamics are usually the ones where investors check how big the market opportunity really is. Growth capital investors know that it is often easier to generate initial traction than to continue growing significantly over a long period of time. Many startups die in the 'growth valley of death' after they have generated initial traction.

Despite the incredible importance of this topic for a growth capital investor's decision to invest in a company, the respective slides often only show huge bubbles with large numbers and a reference to publicly available data. Such slides make growth capital investors skeptical. They either show that you have not analyzed the market properly (and are not as diligent as investors want you to be) or the market is actually not that big at all. Most growth capital investors prefer the bottom-up approach over the top-down approach to market sizing.

Be precise and clearly define your key target customers, show your analysis as to the size of the total addressable market (TAM), the serviceable addressable market (SAM), and the serviceable obtainable market (SOM). Also elaborate on relevant market dynamics.

Competition

Companies have competitors. And investors want to invest in the winner.

Investors need to understand the competitive environment. But even more importantly, they want to understand why they should invest in you and your company. What is your company's differentiator and competitive advantage? Have you built a competitive moat, or will you be able to do so? Examples of competitive moats are resources or partnerships that others do not have, complex technology and respective patents, or network effects that make it unattractive for customers to switch to competitive solutions.

While the section on market size, structure, and dynamics should demonstrate that your company is active in a large market, this section should clearly state how and why your company will win in this market.

Team

Even if you can demonstrate an attractive market and growth opportunity, there will always be execution risk that investors have to assess. Are you and your management team able to pull it off?

Investors look for excellent founders who have the required complementary skills. Founders need to be resilient and persistent. They preferably have relevant industry expertise (sometimes called founder/market fit) and can attract high caliber talents. Eventually, you need to demonstrate your ability to build not only products, but a successful team.

In addition to the members of the management team, you may also provide information on the members of the board of directors and the shareholders in the company.

A fully-diluted cap table showing shareholders with their percentage shareholding and employee stock options that have already been allocated and those that are still available for allocation may complete this section. This will enable investors to assess the capitalization structure risk. They want to understand whether you and your key employees will still be sufficiently incentivized after having raised the growth capital round and potential future financing rounds. If you have pursued the FastScaling approach to growing your business this should be the case. You will have grown your business predictably and cash efficiently and will have faced less dilution than you would have faced if you had scaled more aggressively.

Your Financials

The section showing your company's financials should contain historic financial information, current trading, the financial plan going forward and the company's key performance indicators (KPIs). If you do not want to show your financials on a very granular level in the pitch deck, you can show aggregated numbers. The business plan containing detailed historic information, assumptions going forward, and predictions for the future can be provided in a separate excel file after the investor has confirmed interest in investing in your company.

Financing Need and Use of Funds

The pitch deck should state the amount you want to raise. I recommend you state a specific number. "We are raising $20m in growth capital" is better than talking about a range of $15m to $25m. A specific number demonstrates that you have a clear view of how much cash you need in order to bring your company to the next stage. If you have thoroughly gone through the prediction process described in Chapter 10, you know how much you need to raise in order to get to the next important milestone.

You should also avoid vague statements regarding your determination to raise capital. Brad Feld, the co-founder of Foundry Group and Techstars, says: "When we meet people who say they are 'trying to raise money,' 'testing the waters,' or 'exploring different options,' this not only is a turnoff, but also often shows they've not had much success. Start with an attitude of presuming success.

If you don't, investors will smell this uncertainty on you; it will permeate your words and actions."[58]

You should articulate what the funds will be used for (R&D, sales and marketing, internationalization, hiring key personnel, etc.).

Potential Exit Scenarios

As investors invest in your company only for a certain period of time before they want to exit their investments, you may end the pitch deck explaining potential exit routes and potential acquirers.

Raising What You Need

As you have thoroughly gone through the prediction process explained in Chapter 10, you can talk in a very sophisticated manner and on the basis of comprehensible data points about how much money you need in order to achieve your next milestone. You do not have to talk about ranges but can validate why the actual and exact number you put on the table is reasonable at this point in time.

As a rule of thumb, the money you raise should last for 18 to 24 months. You do not want to start fundraising immediately after the previous fundraising process has closed. You rather want to focus on achieving your plans and the next milestone. If you deliver on your plan and achieve your milestone, you can raise additional money on an even higher company valuation in two years' time.

---

58   Venture Deals: Be Smarter Than Your Lawyer and Venture Capitalist / by Brad Feld and Jason Mendelson.

Agreeing on a Mutually Attractive Company Valuation

There is not one methodology with which all startups are being valued. The valuation methodologies and multiples being used differ from business model to business model, from stage to stage, from market to market, and from investor to investor. You best discuss with your board of directors and major investors the valuation topic. Your board members and major investors look at 'similar' companies all the time and should have many data points as to how 'similar' companies are currently being valued. The valuation range you may jointly define as reasonable in light of your company and market specifics will very likely be a good starting point for your discussions with potential investors.[59]

The only recommendation I have in this regard is that you should optimize your valuation for the long-term, not for the short-term. If you over-optimize your current valuation, this may be attractive for you now. A higher valuation leads to fewer shares being issued to your new investor and logically to less founder dilution.[60] But an over-optimized current valuation may haunt you in the long run. Future investors may not be willing to continue paying valuation premiums. And they may not like to suggest flat or down rounds either. Suggesting flat rounds and down rounds is

---

59 Mark Suster wrote a great piece on how to communicate valuation to investors. You can retrieve his blog post 'How to Talk about Valuation when a VC Asks' here: https://bothsidesofthetable.com/how-to-talk-about-valuation-when-a-vc-asks-7376f5721226 .

60 Certainly, assuming that the investment amount is fixed.

to investors like saying to your existing investors that they paid too much in the last round or did not create value since then. Neither is an attractive proposition in the investor ecosystem where people have to work together many times. You may ultimately end up with an over-optimized current valuation and difficulties finding investors willing to invest in your next financing round. In the long run, you may therefore be better off directly agreeing on a valuation that is attractive for both you and your existing shareholders on the one hand, as well as the new investor on the other hand.

If you strive for and agree on a fair valuation with the investor who suits you and your business best, you are well-positioned to achieve your next milestone and raise your next financing round again on mutually attractive terms. Prioritize personal fit and value creating potential over the valuation offered.

· · · · ·

If you have raised your growth capital round, you can fuel the growth engine and continue FastScaling until you have reached the next milestone and raise additional capital or sell the company. In the next chapter, we will take a closer look at the exit and finding your exit path.

Key Founder Takeaways

☐ If you want to raise growth capital, you need to put yourself into the shoes of your potential growth capital investors and create a pitch deck tailored to their specific interests. Ultimately, their interest is to make abnormal later stage fund returns.

☐ The potential investors need to fit your company and investment stage profile.

☐ While the pitch deck should describe in a compelling way why investing in your company is the right thing to do, you should keep in mind that investors look for founders they can trust and with whom they can build a long and fruitful relationship. You should therefore refrain from overstating important business aspects and focus on establishing credibility by providing a visionary, but authentic, transparent, true, and fair view of your business. Be ambitious, but realistic!

☐ Your pitch deck should touch upon all FastScaling building blocks and also elaborate on potential exit routes that lead to the financial outcome your potential investors target.

☐ The pitch deck should clearly state the amount you want to raise. I recommend you state a specific number. "We are raising $20m in growth capital" is better than talking about a range of $15m to $25m.

☐ As a rule of thumb, you should raise what you need according to your cash flow predictions and what lasts for 18 to 24 months.

☐ I recommend you optimize your valuation for the long-term and avoid over-optimizing your current round valuation. Over-optimizing your current round valuation may haunt you in the long run.

☐ If you strive for and agree on a fair valuation with the investor who suits you and your business best, you are well-positioned to achieve your next milestone and raise your next financing round again on mutually attractive terms.

Finding the Exit Path

Chase the vision, not the money, the money will end up following you.

TONY HSIEH, FOUNDER OF LINKEXCHANGE AND

FORMER CEO OF ZAPPOS

You have worked hard in order to build a massively valuable business. You have gone through sleepless nights, successes, and failures. Blood, sweat, and tears. Now, it is time to harvest and exit your venture. As you have been thoroughly planning and executing your growth strategy, you should not screw up this last step on your growth path, the exit.

Let us therefore look at how you find your exit path and successfully plan and execute your exit strategy.

Finding the Exit Path

There are three typical exit paths.

If all goes extremely well, an initial public offering (IPO) can be an exit option. But you can hardly plan 'to IPO'. It may become an exit option only at the end of your journey where you must weigh all options you have. In order to maximize the exit valuation, you may end up pursuing a so-called 'dual track process' pursuing an initial public offering process in parallel to a secondary transaction or a trade sale process.

Under a secondary transaction, you sell your company or the majority of the shares in your company to a financial investor like a private equity firm. Like your venture capital investors, private equity firms buy to sell. They buy your company, steer it through a period of operational, strategic, and investment performance improvements, and sell it. The ability of private equity firms to achieve high returns can be attributed to such performance improvements, financial and tax engineering in terms of leveraging the acquisition with an aggressive use of debt, focusing on free cash flow and margin improvements, and incentivizing the management of the acquired company towards further increasing the equity value.

FastScaling - On the basis of a relentless and company-wide focus on customer success, product/market-fit, product/channel-fit, strong unit economics, and a scalable technology infrastructure, efficiently and predictably leading and scaling a business fast towards market leadership in a large market.

If you sell your company to a private equity firm, your journey is rarely over. Unless you have already managed to create a top management team that can run the business successfully without your involvement, you will still have to continue steering the business going forward.

As private equity firms focus on maximizing financial returns, they try to 'buy low and sell high'. Correspondingly, the exit valuation you can achieve when you sell to a private equity firm is sometimes significantly lower than the valuation you can achieve under a trade sale to a strategic acquirer.

Under a trade sale, you usually sell 100% of the shares in your company to a large corporation that buys your company for strategic reasons.

Among all exit options, you can best plan the trade sale. All other options usually arise in connection with an actual exit process. Successfully planning a trade sale to a strategic buyer requires you identify your potential acquirers and build relationships with them early on.

Building Relationships with Strategic Acquirers

Chances are high you have already thought many times about who your potential strategic acquirers could be. But I encourage you to discuss with your board of directors and major investors the potential buyer universe on a regular basis. When your investors invested in your company, they had already thought about all exit options and the potential buyers for your business. Together with your board of directors and major investors, you are well-positioned to come up with a pretty good list of companies who could end up buying yours.

M&A advisors and investment bankers can also be a great source of respective intelligence. They will approach you anyway regularly. Take their calls and meetings. A good advisor will not approach you before having thoroughly analyzed the acquirer universe and knowing who you should be connected with.

If you have identified your potential buyers, get in touch with them. Ask your investors, board members and advisors for warm intros to the top management, corporate development, or business development teams. Warm intros matter and improve the chances your counterpart takes a meeting or call.

Before you go into the first meeting or call, be prepared. In the beginning, it is not about the exit. It is about building authentic relationships and often commercial partnerships.

Working with Strategic Partners

It is most important that the right people get to know you and have your company on their radar early on.

But if there is already a strategic fit between your company and a potential strategic acquirer, commercial partnerships like supplier, reseller, or any other form of commercial partnerships can become an option, too. Such commercial partnerships are often pretty intriguing, at least on paper. They often promise both significant new business and a close relationship with a company that may end up acquiring you. But I recommend you carefully assess the pros and cons of entering into a commercial partnership with a potential strategic acquirer.

Sometimes, these kind of cornerstone partners demand you customize your products to their needs. Product customization creates a lot of complexity. If you have pursued the FastScaling approach to growth, you have carefully planned your growth trajectory and your growth engine is running fast and smoothly. If you now have to adjust your products and product features to the needs of just one partner, this usually impacts your product, engineering, and customer success teams who have to additionally work on the 'strategic project'. This requires attention, incurs additional costs, and leads to product, tech, and business complexity that can have a severe detrimental impact on your growth going forward. Think twice before agreeing to product customization. It is a growth killer!

I have also seen strategic partners asking for access to proprietary data. If you generally sell such data to third parties, you can certainly sell it to your partner, too. But, no free lunch or special rights, please! And carefully assess what data you share. If you do also have data about or commercial relationship with competitors of your strategic partner, think twice before sharing respective information. Otherwise, you may end up losing all commercial partners and destroying the relationships you have built with other potential acquirers.

I have also come across corporations who tried to combine their investments with being granted special strategic rights. This usually applies to corporate venture capital units of large corporations. Be careful! Make sure you do not grant any special rights scaring off other potential acquirers from cooperating with you or acquiring you later on. While you may get even closer to one potential acquirer, you must always retain your independence and attractiveness in order to be an interesting target also for other potential acquirers.

If you go as far as accepting an investment from your strategic partner, I strongly recommend you do not grant your potential acquirer any kind of right to acquire your company later on. Such strategic rights can have a material detrimental impact on your potential buyer universe, exit process, and exit valuation.

There are two exit scenarios you can expect to see if you have granted your strategic partner strategic rights like rights of first refusal, call options, and matching rights allowing your partner to become a major or majority shareholder.[61] Firstly, you may end up not being able to generate much interest within the buyer universe because other potential acquirers expect your existing strategic partner to exercise its acquisition right. Secondly, if your strategic partner indicates not being interested in exercising its strategic right to acquire your company, potential other acquirers may wonder why. Ultimately, your existing partner is not only a commercial partner, but also a shareholder with a holistic overview of your business, a well-informed shareholder that decides not to buy. In either case, you can expect to see that strategic rights you have granted to your strategic partner will reduce either the interest in the market or the valuation you are able to achieve when you exit your company.

61   Rights of first refusal are typically granted to all investors. If a shareholder wants to sell its shares, your existing shareholders shall have the first right to acquire them. But rights of first refusal become dangerous if they are granted also in case the majority of the shares are being sold in an exit or if they allow your strategic partner to become a major or majority shareholder.

Getting close to your potential acquirers is smart. But before you enter into any kind of agreement with a potential strategic acquirer, discuss with your board members and major investors the potential impact such relationships could have on your exit path.

Timing the Exit

When is the right time to exit your company? This often depends on internal and external factors.

It may be the right time to exit, if you do not feel the drive and energy anymore that is needed to further scale your business successfully. Together with your investors, you may then decide to sell the company, at least if stepping off and allowing a new CEO to take over is not a better alternative for the company. But bear in mind almost all exit paths entail you stay on board for a certain period of time, unless you have already created a top management team that can run the business without you. This may certainly become part of your exit plan.

Another internal factor can be that you realize you cannot continue innovating and scaling your business. The best time to divest is before revenue peaks and growth slows down. If you sell in the middle of a high growth journey, you are usually able to achieve a higher exit valuation than you would achieve if you sold after growth has slowed down.

As to external factors, attractive public markets may open a compelling exit window in terms of an initial public offering

(IPO). Strategic acquirers may knock on your door and propose interesting terms. Or your investors need to exit in light of their fund lifecycle.

You cannot influence these external factors, but you can be prepared. You can follow the public markets. You can understand the investment horizons of your investors. And you can stay close to your potential strategic acquirers.

If you are prepared, you can proactively initiate an exit at the right time.

Keeping Your House in Order

Being prepared includes keeping your house in order.

When it comes to an exit, you have probably gone through some financing rounds already. In connection with these fund-raising processes, you established a due diligence data room containing all relevant information. Corporate documentation like investment and shareholders' agreement as well as board meeting minutes, documentation related to your intellectual property, financial information like your business plan and key performance indicators, information related to your employees, and important commercial agreements, are but a few examples of information you already gathered.

You have all relevant information in one place. Doesn't this feel fantastic? You can access all relevant company information at the push of a button when you need it from a business intelligence perspective or if an acquisition offer comes out of the blue. I am convinced continuously updating your data room reduces stress and facilitates your exit process. If you can provide potential acquirers with relevant information on short notice, it also conveys a picture of professionalism.

I therefore encourage you to keep your house in order. Make your Chief Financial Offer responsible in this regard and ask her to ensure your C-Levels continuously update their relevant sections of the data room.

Understanding the Interests of Your Acquirer

If you receive an acquisition offer, try to understand the interests of your potential acquirer.

Why do you receive the acquisition offer? Is it because the company wants to recruit you and your team under a so-called 'aqui-hire'? Is the acquirer interested in your products or wants to acquire your revenue? Or is this a defensive move with which the acquirer wants to tackle a strategic threat? What are your potential acquirer's alternatives? Are you just one of many target companies your counterpart talks to? Could your potential acquirer develop the products itself?

It is important you put yourself in the shoes of the acquirer and understand the interests behind the acquisition offer. This knowledge enables you to assess your negotiation power that will ultimately impact the price you can achieve. For instance, you may infer comparable companies are traded on an 8x revenue multiple and, assuming you have $50m in revenue, that this would lead to an enterprise value of $400m. At the same time, your acquirer's willingness to pay may be significantly higher if the acquisition generates substantial synergies or if the opportunity costs of not acquiring your company were substantially higher.

Understand the interests of your acquirer and you are well-positioned to negotiate a great deal and achieve a massive exit valuation.

Engaging Advisors

Should you negotiate the deal yourself or better hire an investment banker to help you sell your company?

It may be tempting to get the deal done yourself, especially if you already have a specific offer on the table. But do not forget your counterpart is very likely a corporate development expert who navigates these kinds of processes successfully on a continuous basis. And she is incentivized to buy your company for the lowest price possible while you want to achieve the exact opposite, the best possible outcome, and a massive valuation. You can therefore expect to encounter difficult negotiation situations in which you may not exactly know how to act and would rather like to have a 'bad cop' at your side who negotiates tough on your behalf. And do not forget you have to run a business successfully in parallel. If the deal does not go through, you do not want to end up with a business weaker than before the process.

Hiring a banker is, as a general rule, a good idea. They help you show your business in the best light possible, structure the deal, manage the due diligence process, and negotiate terms also with multiple potential acquirers. They can be the 'bad cop'. If you want to initiate the exit process without having received an acquisition offer, the banker can also reach out to the whole universe of potential buyers. Ultimately, a competitive process in which a banker is involved has a positive impact on the valuation you can negotiate. When the potential acquirers see a banker is involved, they know the process is very likely a competitive one.

By default, investment bankers can be very helpful in terms of deal making and negotiating attractive terms. But they pursue their own interests, too. They are usually paid only an insignificant monthly fee (the retainer) and charge a high commission on the price for which the company is being sold. While you want them to be incentivized to sell the company, you need to avoid a situation in which the incentives of your banker are not 100% aligned with your interests and the interests of your shareholders. I recommend you therefore discuss with your board members the banker you want to engage and the fee structure.

A great M&A lawyer should supplement your team. Choose a transaction lawyer with great experience in getting deals done. You should personally click with her and she should stand out not only for her legal expertise but also her business acumen. Your lawyer must have a solid understanding of the economics of the deal. She is supposed to be a deal enabler and not a showstopper.

▪ ▪ ▪ ▪ ▪

If you scale your business pursuing the FastScaling approach to growth, you will be well-positioned to sell your company on the basis of a massive company valuation. At the same time, you will have scaled efficiently and retained a major stake in your company. Very smart!

Key Founder Takeaways

☐ As you have been thoroughly planning and executing your growth strategy, you should likewise thoroughly plan your exit.

☐ There are three typical exit routes: an initial public offering (IPO), a sale of the company or the majority of the shares to an institutional investor like a private equity firm, or a trade sale of the company to a strategic acquirer.

☐ Among all exit options, you can best plan the trade sale. All other options usually arise in connection with an actual exit process.

☐ Successfully planning a trade sale to a strategic buyer requires you identify your potential acquirers and build relationships with them early on.

☐ Discuss with your board of directors and major investors the potential buyer universe on a regular basis. M&A advisors and investment bankers can also be a great source of respective intelligence.

☐ If you have identified your potential buyers, get in touch with them. Ask your investors, board members and advisors for warm intros to the top management, corporate development, or business development teams.

☐ It is often very intriguing if a strategic acquirer wants to build a commercial relationship with you. But before you enter into any kind of agreement with a potential strategic acquirer, discuss with your board members and major investors the potential impact such relationship could have on your exit path.

☐ By default, do not grant your potential acquirer any special rights that can scare off other potential acquirers from cooperating with you or acquiring you later on. Retain your independence and attractiveness for other potential acquirers and refrain from granting rights of first refusal, call options, and matching rights that allow your partner to become a major or majority shareholder.

☐ Your exit timing depends on internal factors like your ability and willingness to continue driving growth and external factors like public markets and your investors' investment horizons. You cannot influence the external factors, but you can be prepared and try to understand the external factors.

☐ Being prepared includes keeping your house in order. Constantly update your data room so you have all important information stored in one place that you can access at the push of a button.

☐ It is important you put yourself in the shoes of the

acquirer and understand the interests behind the acquisition offer. This knowledge enables you to assess your negotiation power that will ultimately impact the price you can achieve.

☐ It may be tempting to get the deal done by yourself, especially if you already have a specific offer on the table. But do not forget your counterpart is very likely a M&A expert.

☐ Hiring a banker is, as a general rule, a good idea. They help you holistically in terms of deal making. But they pursue their own interests, too. While you want them to be incentivized to sell the company, you need to avoid a situation in which the incentives of your banker are not 100% aligned with your interests and the interests of your shareholders.

☐ A great M&A lawyer should supplement your team.

☐ If you FastScale, it may take you a bit longer. But the probability that you ultimately sell a massively valuable business is significantly higher.

Please Leave a Review and Spread the Word

I have written this book in order to help founders succeed.

Please help me achieve this goal and create awareness among your peers, founders, and aspiring founders.

Please be so kind to leave a review on Amazon and spread the word on social media and where founders spend time.

I thank you endlessly!

Calculating Unit Economics

n general, the unit economics concept is the same for each and every business and business model. You want to understand the economics of the units you sell. Focusing on the customers you acquire, you want to understand your customer lifetime value, your customer acquisition costs, and your payback period. However, the unit economics are calculated slightly differently depending on the business model you pursue.

Calculating the Unit Economics of Recurring Revenues Businesses

Under a recurring revenues business, the company typically generates monthly recurring revenues (MRR) from its customers until they churn.[62] For instance, in a software-as-a-service (SaaS) business model, the software company licenses its software to its customers on a subscription basis. There are other recurring revenues businesses like infrastructure-as-a-service (IaaS), and platform-as-a-service (PaaS) businesses that exhibit similar characteristics.

---

62   You also encounter companies that charge quarterly or yearly recurring fees.

The beauty of these recurring revenues businesses is that the installed customer base generates a constant flow of recurring revenues that increases as long as the revenues coming from new customers exceed the revenues attributable to customers who churn, i.e. customers who have terminated their contracts and do not have to pay subscription fees anymore. In a recurring revenues business, it is therefore important that founders concentrate on both retaining the installed customer base and acquiring new customers.

In a recurring revenues business, the unit economics are calculated as follows:

Customer lifetime value (CLV) = Monthly Recurring Revenue (MRR) * Contribution Margin (CM) * Lifetime in Months

If you also sell one-off products and services to your customers, you will certainly also have to add the respective product or service contribution to your customer lifetime value calculation (as a one-off addition, but not by increasing the monthly recurring revenue, since the product or service is only sold once and cannot be part of your recurring revenues).

The best way to assess the lifetime of your customers is to look at your customer cohorts that will show how long your customers typically stay with your company (the retention in months). Another way to calculate the lifetime of your customers is to work with your monthly churn rate, i.e. the rate with which you lose your customers on a monthly basis. For instance, if you lose 2% of your installed customer base per month, your churn rate is 2% and the customer lifetime is 50 months (1/2%).

Customer Acquisition Costs (CAC) = (Marketing Costs + Sales Costs)/Number of New Customers Acquired

Payback Period = Customer Acquisition Costs (CAC)/(Monthly Recurring Revenues (MRR) * Contribution Margin (CM))

Very often, recurring revenues businesses have to go through long periods of negative cash flow. They invest upfront in acquiring customers but will recoup such investments only over a certain period of time, the payback period.

For instance, if a company incurs $1,000 in customer acquisition costs in order to acquire a customer with a monthly contribution of $80, it takes 13 months until the initial cash outflow of $1,000 is recouped ($1,000/$80). The initial cash outflow in month one is $920 ($1,000 - $80), while the monthly cash inflow in the following months is 'only' $80.

The more a company accelerates growth and invests in acquiring customers, the greater the company's initial cash outflow and the corresponding upfront financing need. If we continue the example and the company invests $1,000,000 in customer acquisition costs, it acquires 1,000 customers who generate a first month contribution of $80,000. The total initial cash outflow amounts to $920,000 ($1,000,000 - $80,000), while the monthly cash inflow in the following months is 'only' $80,000.

This is where many investors and board members request founders stop further fueling the growth engine. They are scared by the negative cash outflow ahead. But this not necessarily the right advice. If the customer lifetime value sufficiently exceeds the customer acquisition costs, the company pursues a viable business model and will ultimately generate ever more cash inflow from the installed base. The financing need will be reduced accordingly.

If the company in our example continues to invest $1,000,000 on a monthly basis to acquire new customers with a customer lifetime of 50 months, the monthly cash flow turns positive in month thirteen.[63] In month 13, it still spends $1,000,000 on customer acquisition, but it already generates $1,040,000 from the installed base (13,000 customers spend $80). Until the company turns cash flow positive in month 13, it burns a cumulative amount of $5,760,000 ($12,000,000 cash outflow and $7,240,000 cash inflow). After the break-even point, the company adds $80,000 each month to its positive cash inflow and reaches a total cash inflow of $1,000,000 in month 25.

If the company invested even more in sales and marketing, the total cash need would go up initially. If the company doubled its investment in customer acquisition and spent each month $2,000,000 on sales and marketing, the aggregate cash need would increase to $11,520,000 ($24,000,000 cash outflow and $12,480,000 cash inflow). At the same time, it would generate more positive cash flow even faster after the break-even point. It would add $160,000 each month to its positive cash inflow and would already generate $2,000,000 of positive cash inflow in month 25.

This comparison shows that it can make a great deal of sense to further accelerate growth by increasing the sales and marketing

---

63   Assuming that revenues immediately translate into cash.

spend even further, provided, however, that the unit economics work and the company has the money required. The company that invests $1,000,000 in marketing and sales each month needs $5,760,000 in funding and the company that invests $2,000,000 in marketing and sales needs $11,520,000 as an external cash injection.[64]

If the unit economics do not work, you burn cash without being able to turn your business profitable at all. For instance, if the company were able to generate monthly contributions of $15, the unit economics would not work. The customer lifetime value would be $750 ($15 * 50 months), whereas the customer acquisition costs would still be $1,000. You would essentially lose money on each customer you acquire.

If the customer lifetime value insignificantly exceeds the customer acquisition costs, you may acquire your customers profitably. But if you scale your business on the basis of weak unit economics, you will usually experience long payback periods and a correspondingly high cash need. This is one reason why it is so important to focus relentlessly on improving your unit economics.

Calculating the Unit Economics of E-Commerce Businesses

Under an e-commerce business model, you usually sell products to consumers or businesses through an online channel.[65] You

---

64   Disregarding all other cash-relevant transactions.

65   There are certainly also C2B and C2C e-commerce business models.

have monthly cohorts of buyers who buy for the first time in the respective month. Each month you add a new cohort of newly acquired customers who buy for the first time. In a recurring revenues business, your customers 'come back' each month and pay their subscription fees. This is different in an e-commerce business. In an e-commerce business, the customers who purchase in the first month may not come back in the next month. But this does not mean that they have churned and will never come back. They may come back in any of the following months. This difference needs to be considered in the unit economics analysis. Instead of working with a churn rate, you work with the retention rate (RR).

You start your customer lifetime value calculation by calculating the first month average customer contribution (FMACC) in terms of the contributions your customers make on average in their first active month. In order to calculate this first month average customer contribution (FMACC), you analyze your customer cohorts.

Let us assume that your customer cohorts reflect that your cohorts generate a first month average cohort order value of $10,000. If you divide this number by the average number of customers per cohort in month 1, you get the first month average customer order value (FMAOV). Assuming that on average 100 customers were acquired and active in the first month of your cohorts, your first month average customer order value (FMAOV) is $100 ($10,000 first month average cohort order value/100 customers who were acquired and active on average in the first month).

In a next step, you apply your contribution margin (CM) to

this first month average customer order value (FMAOV) in order to get to the first month average customer contribution (FMACC). Your contribution margin (CM) considers your costs of goods sold (CoGS) and all other direct costs like packaging, shipping, and return costs, but not any marketing and sales costs that go into your customer acquisition costs.[66]

If we assume that you can generate a contribution margin of 5%, you get to a first month average customer contribution (FMACC) of $5 ($100 first month average customer order value (FMAOV) * 5% contribution margin (CM)).

Analyzing your cohorts will also help you infer your customer lifetime and your retention rate (RR). If your cohorts show that your customers do not return after four years, your customer lifetime is 48 months. If the cohorts additionally show that your customer cohorts generate on average 20% of the first month cohort order value during months 2 through 48, your cohort order value retention rate (RR) is 20%.

On this basis, you can now calculate the contribution your customers make on average in the period after month 1 (months 2 through 48 in our example). I call this contribution the terminal average customer contribution (TACC).

In our example, the terminal average customer contribution (TACC) is $47 (the first month average customer contribution (FMACC) of $5 * 20% retention rate (RR) * 47 months).

66   It can certainly also be of interest to separately calculate, track, and report your gross margin, your contribution margin (CM1), your contribution margin after marketing (CM2), and your contribution margin after marketing and fixed costs (CM3). Some companies report their margins on an even more granular level.

The total customer lifetime value is the sum of the first month average customer contribution (FMACC) and the terminal average customer contribution (TACC). In our example, the customer lifetime value is $52 ($5 FMACC + $47 TACC).

This translates into the following customer lifetime value formula:

Customer lifetime value (CLV) = First Month Average Customer Contribution (FMACC) + Terminal Average Customer Contribution (TACC)[67]

FMACC = First Month Average Order Value (FMAOV) * Contribution Margin (CM)

TACC = FMACC * Average Retention Rate (RR) * Lifetime in Months after Month 1

As to your customer acquisition costs, you can generally apply the calculation methodology applied for recurring revenues businesses. You divide your sales and marketing costs by the number of customers acquired.

Customer Acquisition Costs (CAC) = (Marketing Costs + Sales Costs)/Number of New Customers Acquired

Very often, e-commerce businesses do not incur sales costs, but only marketing costs, so you end up dividing your marketing costs by the number of customers acquired. If we assume that your company invests $50,000 in marketing and acquires 5,000 custom-

---

67   Alternatively, you could also calculate the average contribution per order and multiply this by the average number of orders done by a single customer over the customer's lifetime.

ers each month, your customer acquisition costs are $10 ($50,000 marketing costs/5,000 customers).

Your customer lifetime value to customer acquisition costs ratio is 5.2 ($52 CLV / $10 CAC).

Your payback period is 10 months. After 10 months your customer contributions amount to $10 ($5 FMACC + 5* ($47 TACC / 47 months)).

Calculating the Unit Economics of Platform Businesses

A platform business *connects* individuals or businesses looking to provide a product or service (supply), with consumers or businesses looking to buy such a product or service (demand). A platform usually takes a percentage commission (take rate or 'rake') on the gross transaction value (GTV).

Platform businesses create repeat business from their customer cohorts and add new customer cohorts each month. But they do not generate recurring revenues like a software-as-a-service (SaaS) business. From a unit economics calculation perspective, platform businesses are therefore closer to e-commerce businesses than to recurring revenues businesses. You can use the e-commerce formulas as a starting point and adjust your calculation to your platform particulars.

In order to calculate your customer lifetime value, you again need to add up your first month average customer contribution (FMACC) and your terminal average customer contribution (TACC). In this regard, you need to especially consider the fact that the platform revenues are not the gross transaction value (GTV) of your platform, but the commission you generate on such gross transaction value (GTV). Revenues are the gross transaction value (GTV) times your take rate or 'rake'.

Your customer acquisition costs can be calculated dividing your sales and marketing costs by the number of new customers you acquire.

While the calculation methodology seems to be straightforward, I have repeatedly seen various inconsistent approaches to calculating unit economics of platform businesses, especially if such businesses collect revenues from only one side of the platform but incur acquisition costs on both the demand and the supply side of the platform.[68]

For example, I have looked at temporary staffing platforms like Shiftgig. Shiftgig may incur costs for acquiring workers (supply), and businesses booking such workers (demand), but only take a commission from the demand side on a shift done by a worker. I have also worked with many catering platforms similar to EZCater. EZCater may incur costs to acquire caterers (supply) and customers (demand), but may only charge a commission on the catering volume delivered. Founders sometimes struggle correctly allocating the costs associated with acquiring the non-paying side of the platform.

I consider such costs product related. For example, on a temporary staffing platform, the workers are more or less the 'products

68   How to Calculate Unit Economics for Platform Businesses / by Patrick Flesner and Richard Meyer-Forsting. Retrieved from: https://www.fastscaling.io/2020/01/02/how-to-calculate-unit-economics-for-platform-businesses/.

and services' being sold and the costs incurred to acquire them are rather 'CoGS' or other direct costs. I therefore suggest you take them into account when calculating your contribution margin (CM) and disregard them when calculating your customer acquisition costs.

If you follow this approach you can adjust the e-commerce unit economics calculation methodology by adjusting the calculation of customer acquisition costs and your contribution margin (CM). The formulas look as follows:

Customer Acquisition Costs (CAC) = (Adjusted Total Sales and Marketing Costs)[69]/Number of New Customers Acquired

Customer lifetime value (CLV) = First Month Average Customer Contribution (FMACC) + Terminal Average Customer Contribution (TACC)

FMACC = First Month Average Order Value (FMAOV) * Adjusted Contribution Margin (CM)[70]

TACC = FMACC * Average Retention Rate (RR) * Lifetime in Months after Month 1

---

69   Adjusted means all sales and marketing costs save for the sales and marketing costs relating to acquiring the non-paying side of your platform.

70   Considering also the costs incurred for acquiring the non-paying side of the platform.

Notes and Resources

Certainly, as a growth capital investor I read regularly about how to grow companies successfully. Below, you find a list of resources that have directly or indirectly found their way into this book.

While I have made every effort to trace the owners of copyright material reproduced in this book, I would like to apologize for any omissions and will be pleased to incorporate missing acknowledgements in any future editions.

Please contact me at fastscaling@fastscaling.io.

General & Introduction

Crawl, Walk, Run / by Fred Wilson. Retrieved from: https://avc.com/2020/07/crawl-walk-run/

The Lean Startup - How Today's Entrepreneurs Use Continuous Innovation to Create Radically Successful Businesses / by Eric Ries

Cash Flow and Destiny / by Ben Horowitz. Retrieved from: https://a16z.com/2013/10/23/cash-flow-and-destiny/

Blitzscaling : the lightning-fast path to creating massively valuable businesses / by Reid Hoffman and Chris Yeh

The pioneers of Silicon Valley's fast culture on how to grow quickly, not recklessly / by Reid Hoffman and Chris Yeh. Retrieved from: https://qz.com/1572866/reid-hoffman-and-chris-yeh-defend-their-book-blitzscaling/

High Growth Handbook: Scaling Startups From 10 to 10,000 People / by Elad Gil.

How to Start a Startup – Why to Start a Startup / by Sam Altman and Dustin Moskovitz. Retrieved from: https://startupclass. samaltman.com/courses/lec01/

The Startup Community Way: Evolving an Entrepreneurial Ecosystem / by Brad Feld and Ian Hathaway

Zero To One – Notes On Startups, Or How To Build The Future / by Peter Thiel

11 Lessons From Venture Capitalist Fred Wilson / by CB Insights. Retrieved from: https://www.cbinsights.com/research/report/ venture-capital-lessons-fred-wilson/

Nail It then Scale It: The Entrepreneur's Guide to Creating and Managing Breakthrough Innovation / by Nathan Furr and Paul Ahlstrom

Generating Product/Market Fit

Can't We Do Better Than NPS? / by Kyle Poyar. Retrieved from: https://openviewpartners.com/blog/cant-we-do-better-than-nps/#. X7ZGky1Q1hG

How Superhuman Built an Engine to Find Product/Market fit / by Rahul Vohra. Retrieved from: https://firstround.com/review/ how-superhuman-built-an-engine-to-find-product-market-fit/

How to Determine Product Market Fit in Your Industry / by Donald C. Kelly. Retrieved from: https://blog.hubspot.com/sales/ product-market-fit

How to make NPS work for you / by Margaret Kelsey. Retrieved from: https://www.appcues.com/blog/nps-score

Moving beyond the Net Promoter Score / by Brian Weinstein. Retrieved from: https://medium.com/@bweinstein/moving-beyond-the-net-promoter-score-9b560f3767ba

Net Promoter Score Considered Harmful (and What UX Professionals Can Do About It) / by Jared M. Spool. Retrieved from: https://blog.usejournal.com/net-promoter-score-considered-harmful-and-what-ux-professionals-can-do-about-it-fe7a132f4430

Net Promoter Score: The Best and Most Humbling Way to Improve Yourself and your Business / by Ha Nguyen. Retrieved from: https://medium.com/speroventures/net-promoter-score-the-best-and-most-humbling-way-to-improve-yourself-and-your-business-382411d030e7

NPS Questions to Gauge Customer Satisfaction [+ Examples] / by Jay Kang. Retrieved from: https://referralrock.com/blog/nps-questions-with-examples/

Product/Market Fit / by Marc Andreessen. Retrieved from: https://web.stanford.edu/class/ee204/ProductMarketFit.html

SaaS startup guide > product/market fit / by Hotjar. Retrieved from: https://www.hotjar.com/grow-your-saas-startup/

Steve Job's Advice on the Only 4 Times You Should Say No Is Brilliant / by Marcel Schwantes. Retrieved from: https://www.inc.com/marcel-schwantes/first-90-days-steve-jobs-advice-on-the-only-4-times-you-should-say-no.html

The Never-Ending Journey: In Search of Product-Market-Fit / by David Skok. Retrieved from: https://www.forentrepreneurs.com/search-for-product-market-fit/

The Never Ending Road To Product Market Fit / by Brian Balfour. Retrieved from: https://brianbalfour.com/essays/product-market-fit

The Startup Pyramid / by Sean Ellis. Retrieved from: https://www.startup-marketing.com/the-startup-pyramid/

What is this Product-Market Fit Thing Everybody Talks about / by Will Herman. Retrieved from: https://medium.com/the-innovation/what-is-this-product-market-fit-thing-everyone-talks-about-a768f3bd7b0d

Why You Should Find Product-Market Fit Before Sniffing Around For Venture Money / by Andy Rachleff. Retrieved from: https://www.fastcompany.com/3014841/why-you-should-find-product-market-fit-before-sniffing-around-for-venture-money

10 Examples of How You May Be Artificially Inflating Your Net Promoter Score® / by Evan Klein. Retrieved from: https://www.satrixsolutions.com/blog/10-examples-of-how-you-are-artificially-inflating-your-net-promoter-score/

12 Things about Product-Market Fit / by Tren Griffin. Retrieved from: https://a16z.com/2017/02/18/12-things-about-product-market-fit/

Generating Product/Channel Fit

Creating Predictable Growth: How to Find Your Product-Channel Fit and Acquire Users That Stick Around / by Kieran Flanagan. Retrieved from: https://learninbound.com/videos/kieran-flanagan-2017/

Product Channel Fit Will Make or Break Your Growth Strategy / by Brian Balfour: Retrieved from: https://brianbalfour.com/four-fits-growth-framework.

The Four Growth Frameworks You Need to Build a $100M Product / by Brian Balfour. Retrieved from: https://www.reforge.com/the-road-to-100m/

The Road to a $100M Company Doesn't Start with Product / by Brian Balfour. Retrieved from: https://brianbalfour.com/essays/market-product-fit

Traction – How Any Startup Can Achieve Explosive Customer Growth / by Gabriel Weinberg and Justin Mares.

Why Product/Market Fit Isn't Enough / by Brian Balfour. Retrieved from: https://brianbalfour.com/essays/product-market-fit-isnt-enough.

5 Steps To Choose Your Customer Acquisition Channel / by Brian Balfour. Retrieved from: https://brianbalfour.com/essays/5-steps-to-choose-your-customer-acquisition-channel

Developing Strong Unit Economics

A Half Dozen More Things I've Learned from Bill Gurley about Investing / by Tren Griffin. Retrieved from: https://25iq.com/2016/10/14/a-half-dozen-more-things-ive-learned-from-bill-gurley-about-investing/

Benchmark General Partner Bill Gurley on Recode Decode. Retrieved from: https://www.vox.com/2016/9/28/13095682/bill-gurley-benchmark-bubble-uber-recode-decode-podcast-transcript

Business Model Analysis, Part 6: LTV and CAC / by Tom Eisenmann. Retrieved from: http://platformsandnetworks.blogspot.com/2011/07/business-model-analysis-part-6-ltv-and.html

Get Out of the ARPU-CAC Danger Zone with Channel Model Fit / by Brian Balfour. Retrieved from: https://brianbalfour.com/essays/channel-model-fit-for-user-acquisition

Higher Growth And Lower CAC - Optimize Your Conversion Funnel! / by Patrick Flesner. Retrieved from: https://www.fastscaling.io/higher-growth-and-lower-cac/

How to Calculate Unit Economics for Platform Businesses / by Patrick Flesner and Richard Meyer-Forsting. Retrieved from: https://patrickflesner.medium.com/how-to-calculate-unit-economics-for-platform-businesses-83c6902d85a1

SaaS Metrics 2.0 - A Guide to Measuring and Improving what Matters / by David Skok. Retrieved from: https://www.forentrepreneurs.com/saas-metrics-2/

Startup Best Practices 13 - Patience with Unit Economics / by Tom Tunguz. Retrieved from: https://tomtunguz.com/patience-unit-economics/

Startup Killer: The Cost of Customer Acquisition / by David Skok. Retrieved from: https://www.forentrepreneurs.com/startup-killer/

Unit Economics: The Vital Signs of Online Marketplaces / by Mike Lloyd. Retrieved from: https://www.linkedin.com/pulse/unit-economics-vital-signs-online-marketplaces-mike-lloyd/

Why Venture Seekers Need a Clear Path to Profitability / by Josh Burwick. Retrieved from: https://www.netsuite.com/portal/business-benchmark-brainyard/industries/articles/cfo-central/unit-economics.shtml

"You need your marketplace unit economics to work" - An interview with Fabrice Grinda / by Mira Muurinen. Retrieved from: https://www.sharetribe.com/academy/marketplace-unit-economics-fabrice-grinda/

10 Marketplace KPIs That Matter / by Andrei
    Brasoveanu. Retrieved from: https://medium.com/@
    algovc/10-marketplace-kpis-that-matter-22e0fd2d2779

Establishing a Scalable Technology

Case studies in cloud migration: Netflix, Pinterest, and Symantec / by
    Chris Stokel-Walker. Retrieved from: https://increment.com/cloud/
    case-studies-in-cloud-migration/

How to Evaluate, Manage, and Avoid Technical Debt / by
    Emmy DeLoach. Retrieved from: https://metova.com/
    how-to-evaluate-manage-and-avoid-technical-debt/

Introduction to the Technical Debt Concept / by Jean-Louis
    Letouzey and Declan Whelan. Retrieved from: https://
    www.agilealliance.org/wp-content/uploads/2016/05/
    IntroductiontotheTechnicalDebtConcept-V-02.pdf

Monolithic Architecture vs Microservices / by Piotr
    Karwatka. Retrieved from: https://divante.com/blog/
    monolithic-architecture-vs-microservices/

The Three Infrastructure Mistakes Your Company Must Not Make /
    by Avi Freedman. Retrieved from: https://firstround.com/review/
    the-three-infrastructure-mistakes-your-company-must-not-make/

The Top 20 Mistakes in Technology / by Seth Hudman.
    Retrieved from: https://akfpartners.com/growth-blog/
    top-20-mistakes-in-technology

The WyCash Portfolio Management System / by Ward Cunningham.
    Retrieved from: http://c2.com/doc/oopsla92.html

What Is Cloud Hosting? / by Kevin Wood. Retrieved from: https://
    www.hostgator.com/blog/what-is-cloud-hosting/

Why startups should run on cloud providers / by Adora Cheung. Retrieved from: https://increment.com/cloud/why-startups-should-run-on-cloud-providers/

10 Benefits of Cloud Hosting / by Kevin Wood. Retrieved from: https://www.hostgator.com/blog/benefits-cloud-hosting/

Striving for Market Leadership in a Large Market

How Sequoia Evaluates Market Size / by Mike Vernal. Retrieved from: https://www.youtube.com/watch?v=ZMPbqLY1wkg

How to Communicate a Startup's Market Size / by Mark Suster. Retrieved from: https://www.youtube.com/watch?v=qW6H92DEGGw

How To Effectively Determine Your Market Size / by Alejandro Cremades. Retrieved from: https://www.forbes.com/sites/alejandrocremades/2018/09/23/how-to-effectively-determine-your-market-size/?sh=334f9ac513d8

Total Available Market (TAM) - Stanford "Strategic Marketing of High Tech and Clean Tech" / by Tony Seba. Retrieved from: https://www.youtube.com/watch?v=_TgVjdxAcf4

Target Big Markets / by Don Valentine. Retrieved from: https://www.youtube.com/watch?v=nKN-abRJMEw

The Value of Knowing Your Market Size / by Kim Moore. Retrieved from: https://www.kgmoore.co.uk/the-value-of-knowing-your-market-size/

Ways to think about market size. / by Benedict Evans. Retrieved from: https://www.ben-evans.com/benedictevans/2015/2/28/market-size

Your market size is only a fraction of what you think it is / by Carl Fritjoffson. Retrieved from: https://medium.com/startup-grind/your-market-size-is-only-a-fraction-of-what-you-think-it-is-f31f79cd1e95

16 More Startup Metrics / by Anu Hariharan, Frank Chen, and Jeff Jordan. Retrieved from: https://a16z.com/2015/09/23/16-more-metrics/

Focusing on Customer Success

Customer Success: How Innovative Companies Are Reducing Churn and Growing / by Nick Mehta, Dan Steinman and Lincoln Murphy

How to Score Customer Health / by Dan Steinman. Retrieved from: https://www.gainsight.com/customer-success-best-practices/how-to-score-customer-health/

Managing Customer Success to Reduce Churn / by David Skok. Retrieved from: https://www.forentrepreneurs.com/customer-success/

Ten Rules for Web Startups / by Evan Williams. Blog post not online anymore

The Correlation between Customer Success and Exit Valuation / by Patrick Flesner. Retrieved from: https://www.fastscaling.io/customer-success-impact-on-growth-and-exit-valuation/

We Start With the Customer and We Work Backward. Jeff Bezos on Amazon's success / by Daniel Lyons. Retrieved from: https://slate.com/news-and-politics/2009/12/jeff-bezos-on-amazon-s-success.html

What Is Customer Satisfaction Score (CSAT)? / by Alex
   Birkett. Retrieved from: https://blog.hubspot.com/service/
   customer-satisfaction-score

Growing Predictably

Introduction to the Sales and Marketing Machine / by David
   Skok. Retrieved from: https://www.forentrepreneurs.com/
   sales-marketing-machine/

Predictable Revenue: Turn Your Business Into A Sales Machine With
   The $100 Million Best Practices of Salesforce.com / by Aaron
   Ross and Marylou Tyler

The Sales Acceleration Formula : using data, technology, and
   inbound selling to go from $0 to $100 million / by Mark
   Roberge

Thinking in Bets: Making Smarter Decisions When You Don't Have
   All the Facts / by Amie Duke

Growing Efficiently

Burn Productivity'... A Consistently Better Signaler of SaaS
   Valuation / by King Goh. Retrieved from: https://medium.com/
   eventuresvc-news/4-burn-productivity-a-consistently-better-
   signaler-of-saas-valuation-33e9d00e02f0

SaaS Economics – Part 1: The SaaS Cash Flow Trough / by David
   Skok. Retrieved from: https://www.forentrepreneurs.com/
   saas-economics-1/

Leading a High Growth Organization

A Guide to Managing Your (Newly) Remote Workers
/ by Barbara Z. Larson, Susan R. Vroman, and
Erin E. Makarius. Retrieved from: https://hbr.
org/2020/03/a-guide-to-managing-your-newly-remote-workers

Entrepreneur Cognitive Bias: 7 Biases That Kill Startups / by
Founder Institute. Retrieved from: https://fi.co/insight/
entrepreneur-cognitive-bias-7-biases-that-kill-startups

Measure What Matters: OKRs: The Simple Idea that Drives 10x
Growth / by John Doerr

Powerful: Building a Culture of Freedom and Responsibility / by Patty
McCord

Trillion Dollar Coach: The Leadership Playbook of Silicon Valley's
Bill Campbell / by Eric Schmidt, Jonathan Rosenberg and Alan
Eagle

6 Proven Business Benefits of Remote Work / by Laura
Spawn. Retrieved from: https://www.cmswire.com/
digital-workplace/6-proven-business-benefits-of-remote-work/

13 Tips For Leading And Managing Remote Teams / by Brent
Gleeson. Retrieved from: https://www.forbes.com/sites/
brentgleeson/2020/08/26/13-tips-for-leading-and-managing-
remote-teams/?sh=6211e136577b

Building a High Growth Organization

Good To Great: Why Some Companies Make the Leap... and Others
Don't / by Jim Collins

The Chief Product Officer vs. The Chief Technology Officer / by Brian de Haaff. Retrieved from: https://www.aha.io/blog/the-chief-product-officer-vs-the-chief-technology-officer

The Sales Acceleration Formula : using data, technology, and inbound selling to go from $0 to $100 million / by Mark Roberge

Creating a High-Functioning Board of Directors

Open-Sourcing the Speedinvest Board Meeting Template - How to Make Your Boards Worth Everyone's Time / by Philip Specht. Retrieved from: https://medium.com/speedinvest/how-to-make-your-board-meetings-worth-everyones-time-21e89b9a3f21

Startup Boards / by Mark Suster. Retrieved from: https://bothsidesofthetable.com/startup-boards-ee3ad0389040

Startup Boards: Getting the Most Out of Your Board of Directors / by Brad Feld and Mahendra Ramsinghani

Raising Growth Capital

How to Start a Startup - How to Raise Money / by Sam Altman, Ron Conway and Parker Conrad. Retrieved from: https://startupclass.samaltman.com/courses/lec09/

Some Advice Before You Hit the Fund Raising Trail / by Mark Suster. Retrieved from: https://bothsidesofthetable.com/some-advice-before-you-hit-the-fund-raising-trail-73dc646f077e

There's No Divorce Clause for Founders and VCs / by Mark Suster. Retrieved from: https://www.youtube.com/watch?v=ybpZMkcm9eM

The 11 Risks VCs Evaluate / by Tom Tunguz. Retrieved from: https://tomtunguz.com/the-11-risks-vcs-evaluate/

Venture Deals: Be Smarter Than Your Lawyer and Venture Capitalist / by Brad Feld and Jason Mendelson

Finding Your Exit Path

Getting to Yes: Negotiating an agreement without giving in / by Roger Fisher and William Ury

Some Quick Thoughts on Exits for Technology Startups / by Mark Suster. Retrieved from: https://bothsidesofthetable.com/some-quick-thoughts-on-exits-for-technology-startups-6029bbb10dcc

Key "M&A takeaways" from the sale of Clustree to Cornerstone OnDemand / by Guillaume Durao. Retrieved from: https://medium.com/@Guillaume_Durao/key-m-a-takeaways-from-the-sale-of-clustree-to-cornerstone-ondemand-308bce968324

What every startup founder should know about exits / by Benjamin Joffe and Cyril Ebersweiler. Retrieved from: https://techcrunch.com/2018/07/31/what-every-startup-founder-should-know-about-exits/

Acknowledgements

I am incredibly thankful for the joy and happiness that I experience every day as an investor working with founders who want to make a difference and change the world. First and foremost, I therefore thank all founders I have been working with for their gratitude for my advice. You make my day. Thank you!

I certainly totally underestimated the work required to write this book. It took much longer than expected. Early and long hours dominated my life for months. I want to thank my family and friends for their support, understanding, and appreciation.

A number of people took the time to review early drafts of this book or specific chapters. An especially big thank you to Kevin Duffy, the co-founder of Winnow, whose feedback has been incredibly helpful and brought this book to a whole new level. I would also like to thank Frank Schlesinger, the CTO of orderbird. Our discussions around technology scalability and your early feedback have been tremendously helpful.

Thanks to Martin Foner for copy-editing and proofreading my self-edited draft. We shared the vision of creating a great book.

Thanks also to Nina Gless. Your design ideas have been a great source of inspiration.

Books are being judged by the cover. Thank you, Vanessa Mendozzi, for having designed the cover of this book. It has been a pleasure working with you and the result is just great.

Thanks to David Miles for designing the book interior. I could not be more content with the outcome of your work.

Special thanks to my lovely wife. Your understanding and constant support have enabled me to write this book.

With this book, I aspire helping not only the founders I personally work with, but all founders who have been brave enough to embark on a risky venture and look for advice as regards how to successfully build a massively valuable high growth business. I thank everyone who helps me achieve this goal by leaving a review on Amazon and spreading the word among peers, founders, and aspiring founders.

I am thankful.

Author Bio

Patrick Flesner is a growth capital investor and a partner at the investment firm LeadX Capital Partners.

Each year, he looks at hundreds of tech companies that want to raise capital in order to accelerate growth. He sees patterns in companies that fail and companies that succeed. His respective growth expertise and his knowledge deriving from more than fifteen years in M&A, Private Equity, and Venture Capital have gone into this book.

Prior to joining LeadX Capital Partners where he built one of the largest European portfolios of B2B tech companies active in consumer industries, Patrick was a lawyer and partner at two German business law firms.

His articles on Venture Capital, Corporate Venture Capital and M&A have been published by renowned magazines like the MIT Sloan Management Review.

Patrick received a Ph.D. in Law from the University of Cologne, and holds a Master of Business Administration (MBA) degree from INSEAD Business School.

Patrick lives with his wife and children in Cologne, Germany.

Made in the USA
Coppell, TX
12 August 2021

60365219R00184